LEARNER-CENTERED PEDAGOGY

LEARNER-CENTERED PEDAGOGY

Principles and Practice

KEVIN MICHAEL KLIPFEL
DANI BRECHER COOK

An imprint of the American Library Association
Chicago | *2017*

Extensive effort has gone into ensuring the reliability of the information in this book; however, the publisher makes no warranty, express or implied, with respect to the material contained herein.

ISBNs
978-0-8389-1557-8 (paper)
978-0-8389-1573-8 (PDF)
978-0-8389-1574-5 (ePub)
978-0-8389-1575-2 (Kindle)

Library of Congress Cataloging-in-Publication Data

Names: Klipfel, Kevin Michael, author. | Cook, Dani Brecher, author.
Title: Learner-centered pedagogy : principles and practice / Kevin Michael Klipfel, Dani Brecher Cook.
Description: Chicago : ALA Editions, an imprint of the American Library Association, 2017. | Includes bibliographical references and index.
Identifiers: LCCN 2016058814 | ISBN 9780838915578 (pbk. : alk. paper)
Subjects: LCSH: Instruction librarians—Training of. | Information literacy—Study and teaching. | Library orientation. | Student-centered learning. | Motivation in education. | Educational technology—Evaluation. | Instruction librarians—Psychology. | Instruction librarians—Effect of technological innovations on.
Classification: LCC Z682.4.I57 K58 2017 | DDC 025.5/6—dc23 LC record available at https://lccn.loc.gov/2016058814

Book design by Kimberly Thornton in the Janson Text and Brandon Grotesque typefaces.

♾ This paper meets the requirements of ANSI/NISO Z39.48–1992 (Permanence of Paper).

Printed in the United States of America
21 20 19 18 17   5 4 3 2 1

CONTENTS

Select worksheets from this book are available for
download at **www.alaeditions.org/webextras.**

Reuben, you'd better leave the game behind and figure out a way to throw some real-live American currency down on the counter. Similarly, all ideas, in the terms of the Pragmatists, must demonstrate their "cash value" by holding up to the ultimate test of empirical reality: how well they help us achieve our goals in our daily practices.

The American Pragmatist philosopher and psychologist William James once said, "Pragmatism is uncomfortable away from facts."[3] So are we. Evidence-based practices, supported by empirical inquiry, are the most secure ways of establishing the kinds of reliable beliefs that help to accomplish the goals we set for ourselves.[4] We can feel safe driving over the Golden Gate Bridge, trust our family MD when we've got a sore throat, and believe that our plane from LAX to JFK will stay in the air because the scientific method *works*. And, in the past few decades, this same methodology has been applied to questions of learning.

This book applies the methodological principles of these established ways of knowing to the information literacy context. "The facts," Carl Rogers said, "are friendly."[5] As librarians, we should find them to be especially so. Librarians are in the business of evidence: we teach learners to locate and evaluate information so they can construct their beliefs in accordance with the best available evidence for a particular claim. In this book, we've done our best to hold our own ideas to these same standards, believing in their value because research indicates that they work and we have found them useful in our own practices.

We'd therefore prefer to think of any theoretical ideas put forward in what follows as a kind of "grounded theory" of learner-centered pedagogy: general principles that have been extrapolated from current empirical evidence about human behavior and can be applied to specific learning contexts. We agree with our library school's philosophy that grounded theory is fundamental for library practitioners to understand. However, as practitioners ourselves, we are ultimately interested in current, empirically validated information that can deliver successful results *in practice*.

Because we maintain a firm foothold in both the theory and practice camps, there's a part of us that approaches offering practical examples with hesitation. On the practitioner side, there can be a natural tendency to only learner-centered pedagogy that you can then apply to your work as library educators. We hope that librarians, after reading this book, will feel more prepared for the changing job market, have more confidence in adapting their skills to the teaching and learning environments of today's libraries, and be well-prepared to facilitate learning environments that result in long-term learning. To this end, this book is meant to function both as an introduction to the theory of and research on learner-centered teaching practices and as a practical guide for implementing these practices in your own work. We believe that reflective practice is the key to our professional success as educators, and in this book we aim to strike a healthy balance between theory and practice.

Methodological Foundations

Over the years, we've noticed that *theory* is sometimes considered a dirty word in our profession. One of the most common complaints we heard as graduate students is that library school focuses too much on theory and not enough on practice. Yet, this focus is not accidental and indeed was stated as the primary focus during our orientation. The library school philosophy seems to be that, though our specific practices will inevitably change, a solid grounding in library science theory and research will help us adapt to a continually evolving professional environment.

We are quite sympathetic to this position; however, we want to be very clear about what we mean by *theory*. Though the theoretical foundations of this book often find their origins in philosophy and psychology, we do not ultimately find any value in such ideas unless they are both empirically supported and can be applied in a practical way. The methodology behind this book is therefore a fundamentally pragmatic one: we are interested in what works in practice. For us, the ultimate arbiter of whether to include any theoretical idea is if it has been demonstrated to facilitate learning. An idea that sounds good in theory but does not help us improve our practices is like trying to buy a sandwich with a pile of Monopoly money. Sure, Monopoly money may be fun to play with, but when it's time pay for your pastrami ingly the case even when instruction was not the primary job responsibility advertised.[1] Due to this change in the hiring landscape, particularly for new and early-career librarians, understanding how students learn is a significant determinant of practical professional success.

Nevertheless, the library school curriculum has been slow to catch up to this trend. Research shows that most ALA-accredited library schools do not require students to take courses in instructional pedagogy or user education. If such classes exist at all, they tend to be offered as electives. Unfortunately, when future instruction librarians do seek out pedagogical training in their MLS program, it is often outdated and inadequate.[2]

The professional transition toward librarians as educators equally impacts librarians who have been working in the field for many years. Though little teaching may have been required when they entered the profession, this expectation now comprises a large part of liaison roles and departmental responsibilities. For practicing librarians to remain current and active contributors to their context, a deep understanding of information literacy and pedagogical knowledge must be added to their repertoire.

Developing this expertise is not only a practical necessity, it is also a professional imperative. Educator and learner-centered-pedagogy researcher Terry Doyle, in his keynote address at the 2014 Library Orientation Exchange (LOEX) conference, challenged instruction librarians to think of developing evidence-based teaching practices as a core professional duty. Just as we might think that surgeons who are not up-to-date on the latest surgical techniques are shirking their professional obligation to their patients, librarians not well-versed in the principles and practice of learner-centered pedagogy fail to hold themselves accountable to their duty as educators. If it is the instruction librarian's job (and increasingly the job of all public services librarians) to help students learn, then we owe it to our learners to teach them in the most effective ways that the literature indicates to us.

Without expertise in the theory and psychology of how students learn, it is difficult to ensure that our practices are ultimately aimed at student learning. But with that knowledge, rather than doing things by feel or past practice, we can feel confident knowing what learning goals we are aiming for and how we can get there. Our goal in this book is to introduce you to a vision of

Pedagogical Expertise and the Current Information Landscape

Now more than ever librarians are required to possess pedagogical expertise. As the profession has begun to transition from classic bibliographic instruction to more conceptually based information literacy curricula, practitioners are increasingly called upon to design, implement, and assess robust reference and instructional practices that contribute to student success. To achieve these goals, and facilitate lifelong learning, librarians must know how to teach information literacy skills that go far beyond a particular library context. In addition to the traditional information expertise of the library professional, today's librarian must also master evidence-based pedagogical practices that can help make learning stick.

Employers have recognized this need and have adjusted their hiring practices accordingly. In a recent study, 87 percent of library supervisors who placed ads on the American Library Association (ALA) JobList for public services jobs indicated that instruction was very important to these positions, and this was overwhelm-

IN THIS INTRODUCTION, WE

- discuss the increased importance of pedagogical expertise for the library professional.

- explain the methodological principles employed in this book.

- provide a road map for each of this book's six chapters.

but I'm glad that I am. And to my mom, who taught me the importance of choosing the right words and sticking with it until it's done.

Billy and Emilia Cook: You are the reason for everything. Love you, my monsters.

Last, but certainly not least, Kevin Michael Klipfel: Five years ago, we sat together in cataloging class, sinking into various levels of despair, and look where we are now. Who would believe it? We wrote a book! Thank you for bringing Carl Rogers into my life, both personally and professionally. It's been a true gift.

December 2016

Sandra Klipfel: Thank you for all your love, support, and certainly not least, devotion to Carolina basketball. I love you, Mom—thank you for everything.

Lastly, to the loves of my life who bring me joy and meaning every day: @ Marlowe_BadCat_LA and L.H.K.: 4.

⊙ ⊙ ⊙

Dani *would like to thank* . . .

This book wouldn't be possible without the influence of my community of friends and colleagues in the library world who have been generous with their time and thoughts: Thank you to Char Booth for giving me my first professional library position and for believing in me, even on days when I was pretty sure that I wasn't up to the task at hand. Cynthia Cohen taught me so much about really and truly listening and helped me think through what I wanted from a lesson plan. Natalie Tagge and Alexandra Chappell: I hope that one day that I can be as fierce and creative as you two. And all the rest of my Claremont colleagues, too numerous to mention, who approach their students with open hearts and minds.

My new colleagues at the University of California, Riverside: In the few short months that we've worked together, you have helped to transform my thinking about library services. Thank you for your honesty, openness, and trust.

While in graduate school, I was lucky enough to be mentored by several amazing librarians and library advocates in a variety of different contexts: Thank you to Rebecca Vargha, Jess Arnold, and Ellie Coen Boote for modeling a person-centered ethos of library work. You continue to influence how I work every day, and I'm grateful to have had the opportunity to work with you all.

Rachel Lewin: My life got infinitely better three years ago, when you moved to Los Angeles. You are the best partner to navigate the world of academia with, and the world of adulthood.

My parents: You were supportive of your overachieving daughter right out of the gate. Thanks, Dad, for modeling for me what it means to be an academic, a parent, and a leader. I didn't mean to follow in your footsteps, neither of us is a Tar Heel born or bred, we both are very proud that one day we will be Tar Heels dead.

We are grateful to Emily Gover, formerly of EasyBib and now of Flocabulary, who was an early reader of our blog and gave us our first big break in her professional development webinar series. She's been a great friend to us over the years, and never less than massively thoughtful.

Thanks to Alex Carroll, a great friend and coconspirator in the library game.

◌ ◌ ◌

Kevin *would like to thank . . .*

Diane Kelly, my advisor at UNC-Chapel Hill, for supporting my master's paper project: your insight and feedback made my work much better, and your support of my coursework in the School of Education made this book possible.

Dani: Thank you for being a wonderful collaborator. But most of all, I've valued the camaraderie and support we've been able to share, from graduate school on through our professional careers. Our discussions always energize me about new possibilities for teaching and learning in our profession, and it's been invaluable to have you to talk to in innumerable other ways.

I've learned an enormous amount about learner-centered teaching and much else from my friend Sotero Vazquez, to whom I give many thanks.

My conversations with Brenda Salley about empathy and authenticity had a major impact on the ideas in this book and also on my life: I really can't thank you enough.

Kevin Shepard: Our relationship has been and continues to be a deeply meaningful part of my life, and I feel grateful to have a place to formally thank you for that. You've influenced this book—but so much more. *We never needed anyone to save us.*

Matt Oremland: Dude, having you as a friend has been one of the luckiest events in my life; thank you for the countless great talks figuring out our lives, your dark humor, and your constant support. "Welcome to."

My grandparents, Sam and Frances Sciolino: I miss you both very much, and it makes me happy to know how cool you would have thought this whole thing is.

ACKNOWLEDGMENTS

This book is the result of more than five years of thinking, and almost everyone we've encountered has influenced it in some way, from the folks at Canter's Deli to our librarian colleagues across the country. We'd like to take a moment to give a shout-out to a few individuals who have made a difference to us over the past five years, and a specific impact on this book in one way or another.

⊙ ⊙ ⊙

Kevin and Dani *would like to thank the following people:*

Our two years in grad school at the University of North Carolina at Chapel Hill were enormously formative for both of us. Many thanks to the faculty and our fellow students at the School of Information and Library Science who both challenged and encouraged us. Gratitude to the staff at the House Undergraduate Library, who gave us jobs, but more than that, gave us the training and trust to teach undergraduate classes while still in graduate school and the freedom and encouragement to explore and experiment for ourselves. Specifically, we thank Emily King, Jonathan McMichael, Suchi Mohanty, and Kim Vassiliadis. Thanks also to Jeff Greene at the UNC School of Education, whose educational psychology seminar opened up a whole world of possibility for thinking about library instruction. Though care about the applications of ideas without understanding their deeper theoretical or empirical justifications. This is understandable since most practitioners are judged either primarily or exclusively on their success as librarians rather than their theorizing about their profession. The danger is that if we ignore the reasons for *why* we do something, then it's hard to know when it stops working well (or at all).

We believe that the value of grounded theory is akin to the value of teaching a person to fish: if you understand how and why a theory helps students learn, you can use your creativity and information expertise to employ it in any number of practical contexts, well beyond the ones we mention in this book. Without that background understanding, you may miss all kinds of opportunities for practical application. So, though we offer many practical examples throughout this book, we consider them useful primarily as demonstrations that these principles can be incorporated, very concretely, into our day-to-day work as librarians. Though you are more than welcome to use any of our strategies in your own context, we believe their value is primarily as inspiration for your own ideas about what might work best for you and your learners.

Road Map

The overall thesis of this book is that learner-centered pedagogy involves taking seriously the idea that *who we are as people matters* in the context of learning. We've organized the book into six main chapters. Each chapter builds on this core idea.

In the first chapter, we introduce a working definition of learner-centered pedagogy drawn from the education literature, counseling psychology, and previous work on learner-centered teaching. We follow the pioneering "person-centered" vision of humanistic psychologist and educator Carl Rogers in placing empathy as central to humanistic education and therapies, by placing the concept of *empathy* at the heart of learner-centered librarianship. We therefore pose, *What is it like to be a person learning something?* as the central question of the book, which we partially answer in each of the following chapters. Finally, we reframe information literacy to be an explicitly learner-centered concept that involves learners using information to think well about what matters to them. This definition of information literacy will inform the practical strategies suggested in the rest of the book.

Chapter two answers the question, What is it like to be a person learning something? from a motivational perspective: what makes a person want to do something, rather than feeling forced? Human beings have an intrinsic desire for autonomy and to express their true selves in their daily activities. One key insight from the current education literature, drawn from several generations of thinking in philosophy and psychology, is that letting students have primary control over the direction of their own learning can greatly improve outcomes. We discuss the research about how facilitating student autonomy and authenticity can lead to increased engagement and motivation as well as demonstrable gains in learning. We then contrast the autonomy-supportive teaching style with a more classic conception of classroom management, the "controlling style," and provide a variety of examples of activities and strategies that support student autonomy in the classroom, at the reference desk, and even in outreach activities.

Chapter three moves away from the affective components of learning to consider what it is like to be a person learning something from a cognitive perspective. Toward this end, we outline six principles from the cognitive psychology literature that librarians can use to organize their information literacy instruction, and we consider concrete examples of how to put these principles into practice. After reading this chapter, librarians will have a solid understanding of what this research tells us about how learners' brains process information and of how instruction librarians can leverage these insights to improve information literacy learning.

Chapter four considers a key element of learner-centered pedagogy, the relationship between learners and educators. Recent research demonstrates that learners learn best from educators with whom they feel an emotional bond. Building on this insight, this chapter situates relationships as a core component of learner-centered pedagogy. We identify a genuine connection between librarian and learner as a catalyst for learning, based on Carl Rogers's counseling principles of empathic understanding, acceptance, and vulnerability, and we outline applications of how to manifest these learner-centered attitudes in practice. We end this chapter by situating our view within the historical tradition known as counselor librarianship.

Chapter five considers issues at the intersection of motivation and cognition. We take educational psychologist Carol Dweck's work on mindset as the starting point of our discussion. Dweck's research shows that students' attitudes and beliefs about learning have a substantial impact on their motivation and ability to learn. It follows, then, that student attitudes about research affect outcomes related to information literacy. This chapter dismisses the myth that intelligence is inherently fixed and provides concrete strategies for creating library learning spaces and instructional approaches that encourage a growth mindset, where students come to believe that, rather than a fixed trait, their abilities can be cultivated and improved through their own choices, effort, and receptiveness to expert feedback.

In the sixth and final chapter of this book, we address the role of technology within learner-centered pedagogy. We outline three main questions librarians can use to test whether using a particular technology for pedagogical purposes could be considered a learner-centered application and discuss several practical case studies to help you consider these questions within the context of your own practice.

Lastly, a brief note on terminology. We prefer the term *learner* rather than *student* because *student* can connote a narrower sense of an individual enrolled in a school or educational institution. Throughout this book, we use *learner* to designate the more expansive viewpoint of a person who is learning something and *student* when we are referring to a learner within a specific institutional context. Learning, curiosity, and exploring questions that matter to us are core elements of being human, no matter where we happen to be placed at a given moment within social institutions. Our use of *learner-centered* rather than *student-centered pedagogy* reflects that distinction as well.

Our primary hope in writing this book is that librarians come away with the confidence to carry out learner-centered practices in their own libraries, even if such practices may go somewhat against the grain of past practice in the library profession. One of the greatest compliments we've ever received on our work came after our presentation, "How Students Learn," at the 2014

LOEX conference, which was in some ways a first draft of chapter three. After discussing cognitive overload and how learners can have a hard time processing too much information, one librarian told us, "I've always felt like I was doing too much in my sessions by trying to introduce students to so many different aspects of the library, but I was always afraid that doing less wasn't the right way to teach." Then this librarian informed us that our presentation gave her the confidence to focus more deeply on conceptual skills in her library instruction. For us, this made our work feel worthwhile. We know how difficult it is to fundamentally change the way you work, and if this book can help give you the confidence and tools to start down the path toward learner-centeredness, then we will consider it a success.

All that said, we certainly don't think the ideas in this book are infallible—any understanding of human behavior will necessarily fall short of that standard—but what we do have is a vision for learner-centered pedagogy grounded in current empirical research on teaching and learning. Our goal is not to convince the skeptic to become more learner-centered, but to help those already inclined toward that direction develop both the confidence and know-how to engage in evidence-based learner-centered practices in their own libraries. Let's do it for our learners: They deserve it.

NOTES

1. R. A. Hall, "Beyond the Job Ad: Employers and Library Instruction," *College and Research Libraries* 74, no. 1 (2013): 24–38.

2. Ibid.

3. W. James, "What Pragmatism Means," in *Pragmatism and Classical American Philosophy: Essential Readings and Interpretive Essays*, 2nd ed., ed. John Jay Stuhr (New York: Oxford University Press, 2000).

4. B. Leiter, "Science and Morality: Pragmatic Reflections on Rorty's" Pragmatism," *The University of Chicago Law Review* 74, no. 3 (2007): 929–37.

5. C. R. Rogers, "This Is Me: The Development of My Professional Thinking and Personal Philosophy," in *On Becoming a Person: A Therapist's View of Psychotherapy*, ed. C. R. Rogers (New York: Houghton Mifflin, 1961), 25.

WHAT IS LEARNER-CENTERED PEDAGOGY?

Defining Learner-Centered Pedagogy

Aside from a few tough cases, you would be hard-pressed to find many educators who don't in some sense identify as learner-centered. Most of us who work in education—whether as teachers, professors, or librarians—pride ourselves on putting students first and aim to make pedagogical choices with the best interests of our learners in mind. Nevertheless, when tasked with articulating the essence of the learner-centered approach, even the most well-intentioned among us may have a hard time clearly expressing what being learner-centered actually means, in a comprehensive sense. So we begin this book by doing just that.

Often, in attempting to define a learner-centered approach, we find ourselves pointing to individual practices or examples of teaching that seem particularly learner-centered. For example, when leading a discussion forum at the 2014 ALA Midwinter Meeting in Philadelphia, Kevin invited the librarians in attendance to share what learner-centered reference librarianship meant to them. The librarians shared strategies that certainly seemed to fit the bill. Many librarians agreed, for example, that helping a student in an academic library conduct research on a topic that interests her is learner-centered, but lecturing students like a "sage on the stage" seems less so. In fact, this group of librarians responding off-the-cuff was pretty intuitively hip to many of the common themes more formally addressed by learner-centered pedagogues within the academic literature. For example, teaching and learning expert Terry Doyle defines learner-centered pedagogy more or less as any practices that involve getting "students to do most of the learning work."[1] Doyle draws this conclusion from contemporary learning sciences research showing that students tend to learn best when their minds are actively engaged, rather than when their teachers are doing most of the talking (and thinking). So the librarians at ALA were absolutely correct: in many learner-centered models of instruction, teachers (and librarians) are positioned as facilitators or guides for learning, rather than pontificating lecturers straight out of *Ferris Bueller's Day Off*.

But though these specific responses strike us as good ones, we want to be careful to avoid concluding that learner-centered pedagogy is simply a set of best practices for the classroom, whether that includes asking students to write about what they are interested in, refraining from being overly authoritarian in lectures, or any of dozens of other strategies that place students at the center of the educational process. These answers are correct as far as they go, but in defining learner-centered pedagogy at the outset of this book, we want to construct a deep, transferable understanding of the concept that takes us beyond a specific strategy to perform or avoid.

In our view, being a learner-centered librarian is about much more than using a particular strategy or gimmick. This book presents learner-centered pedagogy as a way of looking at the world and how we connect to other human beings that has deep implications for the way we practice as teachers and librarians. Our view, simply stated, is that *who we are as people matters*. Our conception of learner-centered pedagogy encourages library educators to encounter the learner as an individual with personal interests, preferences, and motivations, and a uniquely human set of cognitive capacities. We must seek to understand who our learners are, in a deep psychological sense, before we can understand how best to assist them in the research process. It is precisely this process of building connection with our students that, in a learner-centered scenario, situates the teacher as a facilitator for learning rather than an "expert," the more traditional, hierarchical role. Understanding our learners as human beings, ones with enormously complex cognitive, psychological, and emotional needs—and the consequences this understanding has for our practice as librarians—is therefore the overarching aim of this book.

In many ways, we follow in the footsteps of a number of scholars who have approached the practice of teaching through a learner-centered lens. Some of our thinking can be specifically tracked to when learner-centered pedagogy officially emerged as a critical concept for K–12 educators in the early 1990s. At the beginning of the decade, the American Psychological Association appointed a task force to bring together research from psychology, education, and related fields to suggest guiding principles for evidence-based teaching. The resulting report, *Learner-Centered Psychological Principles: Guidelines for School Design and Reform,* began an ongoing conversation among educational practitioners about applying best practices from the literature to the classroom, with theoretical roots going back to creative thinkers such as John Dewey, Lev Vygotsky, Maria Montessori, and Carl Rogers.[2] This book certainly is rooted in the evidence-based tradition of psychology, cognitive science, and education, but our core understanding of learner-centered pedagogy as a deeply humanistic concept is unique among the current learner-centered literature. Since we owe this understanding in large part to our reading of some key humanistic texts, we take a brief tour of the major works that inform this approach and explain why this approach is so relevant to library educators today.

Carl Rogers and the Importance of Empathy

The view of learner-centered pedagogy in this book owes its greatest debt to the humanistic tradition in psychology and education, and we're particularly indebted to the "person-centered" approach of the psychotherapist and philosopher of education Carl Rogers. One of the most influential figures in the Humanistic Psychology movement of the 1960s, Rogers initially rose to prominence in the world of counseling and psychotherapy, not in the world of education. He made his name by defending the seemingly simple belief that human connection is at the heart of psychology. Rogers believed that, given the right conditions, everyone can reach their true potential as human beings, just like a plant given the appropriate amount of water and sunlight will naturally grow and flourish. He hypothesized that human beings have an innate desire to express themselves, an intrinsic need to connect in positive ways with others, and a desire to actualize themselves in the world in a constructive manner. Things go awry, however, when in the process of developing into adults, we receive messages and internalize values that run counter to our understanding of ourselves as individuals. Many of our dominant psychological strategies for raising children, Rogers thought, are the psychological equivalent of systematically pouring a quart of motor oil onto a baby avocado plant and expecting it to grow into a healthy, fruit-bearing tree.

That Rogers's views may now strike us as fairly commonplace only demonstrates how deeply the humanistic mindset has become ingrained in our current cultural understanding of human behavior.[3] In the '60s, Rogers's theories were considered quite radical since they fundamentally challenged the dominant theory and practice of psychotherapy of the day, Freudian psychoanalysis. For the practicing Freudian, the therapeutic process was an impersonal one; it was clinical and inegalitarian in the same way that many contemporary encounters with physicians still tend to be.

For example, let's imagine that you have a pain in your ear so you make an appointment with your doctor. It would not be unusual for the doctor to enter the examination room with a cursory greeting, move directly to looking in your ear, say something along the lines of, "Yup, you have an ear infection," and proceed to typing out a prescription before quickly exiting the room. This process, at its core, requires no meaningful relationship building or personal connection between physician and patient; it simply involves an individual with a general sense that he might be sick consulting with an expert who employs her superior understanding and training to effect a cure.[4]

In a similar manner, in traditional Freudian psychoanalysis, a psychological expert listens to a troubled person with the goal of objectively understanding the individual's difficulties. The psychoanalyst then applies his vast psychological knowledge to interpret the patient's past, thereby "curing" her of suffering. The psychoanalyst's expertise is at the core of the interaction, with his superior knowledge leading to a cure for the individual's distress. And, at least on the surface, this seems to make an awful lot of sense. After all, why go see a therapist if not for the therapist's superior psychological knowledge?

Rogers's controversial response, which he outlined in his seminal 1957 paper, "The Necessary and Sufficient Conditions for Therapeutic Personality Change," was that the therapist's psychological knowledge and authority have absolutely nothing to do with whether or not a patient gets better.[5] Instead, what actually helps an individual make a constructive personality change that leads to increased happiness is the *therapeutic relationship:* the connection that the client feels with his therapist, and the degree to which he feels personally understood.

Given this insight, Rogers came to realize that what mattered was not the therapist's abstract knowledge of psychology, but the ability to accept patients for themselves. If the primary cause of human suffering is an individual's feelings of rejection, then it is the psychologist's job to manifest the opposite attitudes toward the patient. Since many individuals' emotional pain is due to having "conditions of worth" placed on them by parents or loved ones (e.g., "behave in this way and I will value you; if you don't, I won't value you"), the therapist must create relationships with patients so that they feel valued unconditionally (what Rogers calls unconditional positive regard).

A central element of Rogerian therapy then becomes the therapist's ability to empathize so that the patient feels understood. For this reason, Rogers coined the phrase *person-centered therapy* for his unique approach to counseling. For the person-centered therapist, an empathic relationship is critical for a person to develop into a healthy individual, with a capacity for autonomy, self-direction, and establishment of genuine and meaningful emotional connections with others. Unlike the Freudian psychoanalyst, the person-centered therapist's aim is not to diagnose a patient and prescribe a cure. Instead, the person-centered therapist's goal is to understand the inner world of another person. It is this empathic understanding, when perceived by the patient, that ultimately helps her develop a secure sense of self.

Thus, for the person-centered therapist, What is it like to be this person? is the central question of the therapeutic encounter. Unlike a general medical practitioner, who can offer an objective diagnosis within a few seconds and then walk away, the successful therapist must create real human connection and authentic engagement with individuals to effect growth and personality change. The foundation of this connection is emotional honesty between the patient and therapist, which requires empathy. Empathy—the ability to understand what it is like to be another person from that individual's point of view—and the ability to accept a person without the desire to change him is a profound facilitator of psychological change. To Rogers, the ideal therapist is one who embodies this empathic mindset toward clients and who practices empathy as a "way of being." In the post-Rogerian world of therapy, simply bringing psychological expertise to the table is no longer enough, and no longer as important as it once was.

In sum, Rogers thoroughly changed the way that psychologists viewed their work—from a highly clinical endeavor to a helping relationship. For us, though, the most interesting part of Rogers's work on person-centered-ness and empathy is that it extends beyond the therapeutic relationship to other domains, such as education. We explore this development in the next section.

A Humanistic View of Education

One reason that Carl Rogers continues to be an important humanistic thinker is that he explicitly extended his insights from the therapeutic setting into the educational realm, and many of his (at the time, radical) hypotheses about education have proven to be empirically sound. Rogers viewed the counseling-patient relationship in person-centered therapy as a learning one because it involves a change in the patient's self-understanding, which is a very common definition of learning and one that we discuss in more depth in the next section. Consequently, Rogers saw no reason that the insights into human behavior and motivation he gleaned from counseling should not transfer into a similar context of learning, the classroom setting.

It follows, then, that in Rogers's view a major part of the educator's job is to facilitate "significant learning" akin to the existentially meaningful, personal kind of learning that goes on in a productive therapeutic relationship. For Rogers, learning takes place on a continuum of meaning. On one end of the spectrum is learning that has no personal meaning to the student, as in the rote memorization of nonsense syllables. Because there is no concrete or compelling personal reason to remember these things, they tend to be forgotten quickly. Unfortunately, Rogers theorized, most of what is taught in a classroom falls into this category since concepts tend to be introduced without context or existentially relevant connection to the lives of the learners.

On the other end of the Rogerian continuum of meaning lies significant learning, which has both meaning and personal relevance to the learner. Significant learning takes place for the learner if, and only if, the learner attaches some personal meaning to the subject of inquiry and wants to learn about the subject matter. Real, genuine curiosity is central to this kind of learning. Significant learning tends to last because the learner is invested in it, and it is precisely this sense of personal meaning, ownership, and caring about what is learned that establishes its relevance to the learner.

Facilitating significant learning—learning that matters to the student from her own point of view—is, therefore, the primary task of the "learner-centered educator." It relies on the same underlying principles of empathy as Rogerian therapy, essentially asking the teacher to put himself in the shoes of the student to create the conditions for lasting learning.

Roger's 1974 article, "Questions I Would Ask Myself If I Were a Teacher," stands as one of his most important pieces in the philosophy of education and expands this idea.[6] It also provides the key foundations from which we've derived our own learner-centered approach. In this piece, adapted from a lecture that Rogers gave to a group of educators, he raises several thought-provoking questions that arise when he applies his person-centered views to the realm of education. Given our understanding of the fundamentals of Rogers's views, it should not surprise us that the framing question of Rogers's article is, What is it like to be a person learning something? Rogers, we learn, places empathy not only at the heart of counseling and psychotherapy, but at the heart of teaching and learning as well.

From this Rogerian question you could basically draw a straight line to how we define learner-centered pedagogy in this book: a way of thinking about education that centrally locates the learner as an individual with unique interests and concerns, which asks teachers to continually ask the empathic question, What is it like to be a person learning something? We take this Rogerian conception of education and learner-centered teaching forward with us in the rest of this book and examine each learner-centered pedagogical choice that we discuss through this lens. But before moving on, we need to clarify another concept central to the rest of this book, by establishing a clear, concrete, and precise definition of learning itself.

What Is Learning, Anyway?

We know, given our discussion of Rogerian pedagogy in the previous section, that facilitating significant learning is at the heart of our notion of learner-centered pedagogy. But this understanding raises further questions: How do we know when significant learning has occurred? What factors serve as objective indicators that we've done our job, facilitating a learning experience where students have come to understand something that matters to them?

To answer these questions, we need a clear working definition of learning and how it can be measured. Otherwise, how will we know what we are aiming for? For the purposes of this book, we define *learning* using one of the most widely accepted definitions in educational psychology: "a [permanent] change in a person's knowledge."[7] Recall from a few pages ago that Rogers considered the counseling-patient relationship in person-centered therapy to be a learning one precisely because it involves creating a permanent change in the way an individual views the world. Were we to add the Rogerian conception of significant learning to this common definition, we might further say that learning involves a *meaningful* permanent change in a person's knowledge.

This change can be measured using two specific metrics, *retention* and *transfer*.[8] Retention refers to a person's ability to remember knowledge and recall it when necessary. For example, before Dani had a baby, she had never changed a diaper in her life. But she knew it was going to be important, so she watched a bunch of YouTube videos, followed some step-by-step tutorials using a Cabbage Patch Kid, and eventually memorized the steps that go into a successful diaper change. Almost a year later, she still has this knowledge and uses it several times a day, so it's fair to say that she *retained* this bit of information. She doesn't need to look it up anymore; it's just something that she knows how to do without even really thinking about it. In the technical language of cognitive psychology, Dani's brain took in this information through her working memory—what is currently before one's mind in the present moment—and stored it in her long-term memory—the part of the brain that holds all the information we've retained until it's ready to be brought back to our working memory for later use. So, when you memorize something and are later called upon to produce that knowledge, it's a simple example of retention in action. And we might consider this a case of meaningful—or significant—retention since without this information Dani would have a smelly and unhappy baby with a bad rash, so she *cares* about knowing it.

Transfer, our second metric of learning, is the ability to take the knowledge learned in one context and apply it to a new situation. The ability to recognize new situations where knowledge applies is the critical-thinking component involved in transfer. For example, if you learned how to calculate the velocity and trajectory of a cannonball in physics class, when you were confronted with a new problem involving where a football will land, you would (if you can transfer) recognize that the same methodology is necessary and apply it to the new context. You took the core knowledge you retained from physics class, critically reflected on it, and used that knowledge to solve a new, seemingly unrelated problem. But since this knowledge may not be all that significant to people who are neither pirates nor NFL players, it may be useful to consider an additional example of transfer.

Kevin recently had a friend bring him an old 35 mm film camera he'd inherited from his grandmother and, since Kevin is passionate about photography and loves old film cameras, asked if Kevin could show him how to load film into the camera. Kevin initially had no idea if he'd be able to show his friend how to do this. The camera, a Praktica FX 2 from the 1950s, was one he'd never seen before and looks cosmetically very different from the 35 mm cameras he's accustomed to using. Yet, despite these differences, Kevin was very quickly able to show his friend how to load the camera. Rather than just knowing how to load film into one camera (his own Leica M3), Kevin could extrapolate the core tenets of loading film into almost all 35 mm cameras and transfer that knowledge to load a strange-looking camera he'd never seen before. This illustrates significant transfer, which is a central component of learning and critical thinking.

We hope that thinking about learning in this way will feel intuitive and familiar to you and that you can imagine your own personal examples of how these concepts play out in your life. We'll use these definitions of retention and transfer to ask two guiding questions that will inform the way we approach our teaching, aimed at maximizing these two learner-centered outcomes:

1. How can I teach so that learners *retain* meaningful information being presented?
2. How can I teach so that learners can *transfer* meaningful information to new contexts?

Whether you are writing a half-sheet how-to on the library's new discovery layer, teaching a one-shot session, designing an online tutorial, or constructing the syllabus for a semester-long information literacy course, keeping these two questions at the forefront of mind can focus your efforts on evidence-based practices that can lead to long-term learning.

Reframing Information Literacy as a Learner-Centered Concept

Having defined both learner-centeredness and learning, we can now turn our attention to how all of this specifically applies to the library context.

Let's begin with some brief history to frame where we are. Though instructing users in how to navigate libraries may be about as long-standing as the institution itself, *information literacy* has a much more recent history. Indeed, the term was first introduced in a 1974 report for the National Commission on Libraries and Information Science by Paul G. Zurkowski. In this paper, he describes information literate people as those "trained in the application of information resources to their work . . . [who] have learned techniques and skills for utilizing the wide range of information tools as well as primary sources in molding information solutions to their problems."[9] Zurkowski estimates that only about one-sixth of the American public could be considered information literate and calls for the commission to embark on a universal information literacy campaign, to be completed by 1984. Needless to say, the admirable-but-lofty goal of universal information literacy was not met by 1984.

In 1989 the ALA Presidential Committee on Information Literacy defined information literacy as the "set of abilities requiring individuals to recognize when information is needed and have the ability to locate, evaluate, and use effectively the needed information."[10] This definition was adopted by the Association of College and Research Libraries (ACRL) as part of the *Information Literacy Competency Standards for Higher Education* in 2000.[11] Fifteen years later, ACRL redefined information literacy as part of the *Framework for Information Literacy for Higher Education,* calling it "the set of integrated abilities encompassing the reflective discovery of information, the understanding of how information is produced and valued, and the use of information in creating new knowledge and participating ethically in communities of learning."[12]

Over the past forty-plus years, we've seen a rhetorical move from using information to solve specific problems to a more theoretical and conceptual understanding of information creation and use. This complicates our understanding of information literacy by focusing less on the results of research and more on the process. In many ways, information literacy has become a more humanistic concept, taking into account how and why information is produced and used.

Considering this history and the evolution of the concept of information literacy, what might an explicitly learner-centered conception of information literacy look like? Keep in mind, because learning involves retention *and* transfer, our information literacy definition should allow for most, if not all, current and future instantiations of information literacy standards our profession happens to come up with. And, at least as important, it must consider significant learning as fundamental to its outlook. Thus, if we take research to be, at its core, an occasion to investigate something that you would personally like to know more about, facilitating this type of learning is the ultimate goal of any particular set of information literacy standards. So, for the purposes of this book, we can define *learner-centered* information literacy as the set of skills allowing learners to use information to think well about what matters to them.[13] While this definition certainly has connections to the ACRL *Framework for Information Literacy*, it allows for a more individualized understanding of how people encounter information and encourages librarians to take an empathic approach to learners—what "thinking well about what matters" looks like might vary greatly depending on the individual. Not only must librarians engage with the learner's curiosity, but also teach learners to think critically about what they find.

By this point, we're sure you won't be all that surprised that this conception of information literacy is drawn from Rogers and the humanistic tradition (as well as a large body of empirical research in contemporary educational psychology that we explore in the rest of this book). Indeed, one of the most striking aspects of Rogers's philosophy of education is how centrally he locates what we might think of as traditional librarian functions within learner-centered pedagogy. In "Questions I Would Ask Myself If I Were a Teacher," Rogers states that perhaps the single most important task of the learner-centered educator is to provide students with resources. Rogers goes so far as to say,

> I believe that a good facilitator of learning should spend up to 90% of his preparation time in making resources available to the young people with whom he or she works. To a large extent [. . .] it is not necessary to teach them, but they do need resources to feed their interests. It takes a great deal of imagination, thought and work to provide such opportunities.[14]

This passage ought to be music to any librarian's ears! All in all, written almost forty years ago without librarians in mind, this sounds very similar to the work that contemporary librarians consistently engage in. Almost every librarian spends a significant amount of time selecting and preparing resources intended for library users. So on the one hand, the learner-centered educator's primary role is to help learners think well about what matters to them, and on the other hand, they must also help learners develop the skills to find quality resources in a meaningful way. The profession has naturally started to evolve toward the Rogerian view of the learner-centered teacher.

What's more, taking the passage from Rogers at face value, thinking about the centrality of resources comes as nothing new to librarians. In his foundational 1931 text, *The Five Laws of Library Science*, S. R. Ranganathan proposes the second law of librarianship as "every person his book."[15] While we tend to focus our understanding of this core professional tenet on implications for collection development, such as considering the unique needs of a community and individuals when building a collection, we can also take it to have more expansive meaning for work in instruction, reference, and outreach. "Every person his book," we suggest, comes from the humanistic assumption that who we are and what we bring with us into the library (or anywhere) *matters* and that our job as experts in finding resources is to connect individuals with materials that will resonate with them and to help learners develop skills to find and recognize quality resources on their own. Indeed, to find every person his book (and, conversely, every book its reader), librarians must employ a practice of empathy to try to understand what motivates individuals and to discover their needs. A learner-centered ethos in the Rogerian mode, then, is basically *built in* to our contemporary understanding of librarianship.

We have extracted two major components of learner-centered pedagogy from Rogers's view of education that we apply to librarianship:

- authentic learning: the need for the facilitator of learning to discover learners' interests and allow them to pursue those interests
- resource provision: the need for the facilitator of learning to provide learners with the resources and materials necessary for them to explore and learn about their interests

The conjunction of these two core ideas provides the basis for our thesis that *information literacy involves thinking well about what matters.* When we combine this understanding of information literacy with the definition of learning borrowed from educational psychology, we see that information literacy educators aim to facilitate educational experiences that help learners develop the ability to retain and transfer these two applied concepts across a multitude of contexts. As we see it, information literate individuals possess a kind of practical wisdom that allows them to successfully use information to pursue their curiosities no matter the context of their information needs.

This is a point worth stressing, as it helps us to clearly delineate the goals of information literacy education. Although much information literacy instruction takes place within academic or public libraries, the goals of information literacy education are much broader than navigating those specific information contexts. Indeed, both Kevin and Dani would be extremely disappointed if the information literacy knowledge that our learners gained during academic research instruction was not directly applicable to thinking well about information in areas of their lives outside the immediate academic context. As librarians, of course we want to and do teach people how to identify scholarly sources, access them through the Open Web and library databases, and cite information appropriately and ethically. But that is only part of learning—it's all retention and no transfer.

We conceive of the teaching librarian's job as something bigger than that: to teach information literacy skills that are applicable in contexts as varied as gathering information for on-the-job decision making, separating fact from fiction during a presidential debate, or simply figuring out which Yelp reviews give an accurate assessment of the best Italian restaurants to eat at in Los Feliz. For true learning to take place, both retention and transfer must be our pedagogical goals, and to make learning significant, personal connection and meaning must be part of the equation. Lifelong information literacy learning—where individuals consistently use information to formulate beliefs about things that matter to them in accordance with the best available evidence—demands no less of us.

Given this understanding, it may come as no surprise that we believe quality information literacy education to be no simple task! However, we are confident that by following a learner-centered path, teacher-librarians can make positive and significant strides toward promoting information literacy. Our goal throughout the rest of this book is to explore concrete, data-driven answers that give librarians practical strategies to deliver successful information literacy instruction. By doing so, we can help learners think well about the things that matter to them, in a way that situates who we are as human beings centrally within the pedagogic process. In the rest of this book, we unpack the question, What is it like to be a person learning something? in a variety of ways and apply it to the information literacy context.

NOTES

1. T. Doyle, *Learner-Centered Teaching: Putting the Research on Learning into Practice* (Sterling, VA: Stylus, 2011), 7.

2. Learner-Centered Principles Work Group of the American Psychological Association's Board of Educational Affairs, *Learner-Centered Psychological Principles: A Framework for School Reform and Redesign*, revised November 1997, www.apa.org/ed/governance/bea/learner-centered.pdf.

3. J. Grogan, *Encountering America: Humanistic Psychology, Sixties Culture and the Shaping of the Modern Self* (New York: Harper Perennial 2013).

4. K. J. Schneider and O. T. Krug, *Existential-Humanistic Therapy* (Washington, DC: American Psychological Association, 2010), 34.

5. C. R. Rogers, "The Necessary and Sufficient Conditions of Therapeutic Personality Change," *Journal of Consulting Psychology* 21, no. 2 (1957): 95–103.

6. C. R. Rogers, "Questions I Would Ask Myself If I Were a Teacher," *Education* 95, no. 2 (1974): 134–39.

7. R. E. Mayer and M. C. Wittrock, "Problem Solving," in *Handbook of Educational Psychology*, ed. P. A. Alexander and P. H. Winne (New York: Routledge 2006), 289.

8. Ibid.

9. P. G. Zurkowski, *The Information Service Environment Relationships and Priorities*, related paper no. 5 (Washington, DC: National Commission on Libraries and Information Science, 1974), http://eric.ed.gov/?id=ED100391.

10. American Library Association, *Presidential Committee on Information Literacy: Final Report*, January 10, 1989, www.ala.org/acrl/publications/whitepapers/presidential.

11. Association of College and Research Libraries, *Information Literacy Competency Standards for Higher Education*, 2000, www.ala.org/acrl/standards/information literacycompetency.

12. Association of College and Research Libraries, *Framework for Information Literacy for Higher Education*, February 2, 2015, www.ala.org/acrl/standards/ilframework.

13. We've borrowed this important phrase, "thinking well about what matters," from philosopher George Hole's book on the philosophy of critical thinking. G. T. Hole, *Thinking Well about What Matters* (Minneapolis/St. Paul, MN: West, 1993).

14. Rogers, "Questions I Would Ask," 137.

15. S. R. Ranganathan, *The Five Laws of Library Science* (Madras, India: Madras Library Association, 1931).

CURIOSITY AND LEARNING

The Importance of Authenticity and Autonomy

Alienation: The Enemy of Motivation

When Kevin was in high school he had an experience that permanently shaped his views on education. During his junior year, Kevin's English class engaged in a major research project that took up a significant portion of the school year. A librarian was enlisted, and many hours were spent in the library mulling over the finer details of MLA citation format. Finally it was time to select a topic, and the teacher presented the class with a list of general questions to choose from. Kevin chose a question from the list and informed the teacher of his intentions: "I'm going to do the one about researching the biography of an influential historical figure: Johnny Rotten." Kevin chose this topic because he'd read Rotten's autobiography so many times that its spine was completely broken.

To put it mildly, Johnny Rotten was not the type of "important" historical figure Kevin's teacher had anticipated students would write about. Johnny Rotten was the stage name of John Lydon, the lead singer of the enormously influential English punk band the Sex Pistols, perhaps most famous for spitting on stage, swearing on live television, and penning a tune about his desire for anarchy in the United Kingdom. However, along with other groups, such as New York City's Ramones, the Sex Pistols are largely credited with ushering in punk rock in the late 1970s.

John Lydon's iconic historical status is confirmed by a present-day catalog search of both Kevin and Dani's workplaces, which hold numerous titles about the cultural legacy of the Sex Pistols and punk rock more generally. Nevertheless, according to Kevin's English teacher, Johnny Rotten wasn't going to cut it for this assignment. The assignment wasn't to write about someone *Kevin* thought was important: This was supposed to be *research*, the teacher said, so he had to choose something *scholarly*. Dutifully, Kevin chose another topic to write about, implicitly learning that there was a clear difference between the things he was interested in and the things that were deemed school-worthy for research projects. This distinction caused Kevin to believe that who he was as a person did not matter in the context of his schoolwork and resulted in a significant decrease in his motivation throughout the rest of his high school career, leading to difficulties with his teachers and parents and his decision not to go to college after high school.

It wasn't until many years later, while attending library school, that Kevin came to recognize this experience as a transformational event. As a student at Carolina, Kevin constantly felt that, unlike the other students at the school, he didn't really belong there. Nearly every morning, as he walked across Franklin Street onto the historic campus, he couldn't help but think about how crazy it was that he was there. I've been a terrible student my whole life, Kevin thought, I barely graduated high school. How do they let me go to school here? This phenomenon is so pervasive that psychologists have named it the impostor syndrome: the fear of not measuring up to others and being exposed as a fraud.

But, in spite of his fears, Kevin took a graduate seminar in the contemporary American novel "for fun" while at Carolina. One day Kevin was in his professor's office discussing his final research paper, which could be on any topic somehow related to the themes in the seminar. For much of the semester, Kevin had been thinking about the debate between the novelists David Foster Wallace and Bret Easton Ellis, with a particular interest in why Ellis had such strong feelings against the "sentimentality" of Wallace's fiction. At some point Kevin's professor said, "Well, I think Bret's just a punk rocker, really. That could be a cool topic for you: the influence of punk rock on the worldview of his novel, don't you think?"

Kevin was floored. He'd gone into office hours planning to discuss "school-sounding" ideas like the nature and purpose of the American novel, and here was his professor telling him that instead he should explore his interest in Bret Easton Ellis and punk rock! Kevin subsequently went to the library, checked out dozens of books on punk rock, and wrote a paper about how punk illuminated certain existential themes in Ellis's work.

One key point that Kevin took away from this experience is the realization that though there were times that he had been a bad student, he'd never been a bad *learner*. Even during his worst student days, he was always enormously interested in ideas. At night, he would read about any number of topics that held his interest but always had a clear sense that none of it had anything to do with school. And in some ways, Kevin was right: far too often school isn't about *you* and the things you care about. It wasn't about your passions or desires or your interest in Johnny Rotten. What did it matter that you'd read a book so many times it fell apart? That was something you could do on your own time; school was a place where the teachers had something to tell you, and it was your job to listen.

These two incidents stuck with Kevin. The juxtaposition between his two English teachers—one who implicitly told him that *who he was as a person* was irrelevant to his education and one who asserted that who he was as an individual mattered within the context of his schoolwork—left a lasting impression. It became a foundational element of Kevin's conception of the kind of educator that he wanted to be.

We start this chapter with Kevin's story because it sheds light on the essential connection between motivation and learning. His sense of alienation from school came about precisely because two things that naturally belong together—personal curiosity and learning—had become unnaturally separated. Kevin's sense that school wasn't about who he was, but instead was about following rules laid down by the teacher, killed his motivation. And, in the story, motivation went hand-in-hand with learning since a personal connection between who he was and the external task he was required to perform was integral to his feeling motivated. When Kevin felt that who he was as a person mattered within the school context, his motivation to learn increased, and when who he was as a person was considered irrelevant within the school context, his motivation significantly decreased. Teachers who facilitated a process of significant learning—knowledge that carries a sense of existential importance for the learner—had a major impact on Kevin's educational experience.

And as it turns out, this is no accident. There is a large body of literature, in fields as diverse as moral and existential philosophy, counseling psychology, and the psychology of education, that confirms this seemingly simple fact about what it means to be a person: human beings have an innate desire to be themselves, and when they can do so, good things tend to follow. In the rest of this chapter, we outline the history of this thinking, discuss its relevance to education, and give specific examples of its applications to the library and information literacy instructional context.

Authenticity and Motivation

Our focus in this chapter is on motivation—the extent to which a person *wants* to do something—because, as we saw in Kevin's case, a learner's motivation heavily impacts how much he learns. Motivation has been tied to numerous classroom outcomes, ranging from the grades students receive to general knowledge acquisition to intellectual development more broadly. If our goal, basically, is to ensure that students are learning, then we need to pay close attention to motivation. When considering motivation from a learner-centered perspective, we begin by returning to the book's central question introduced in chapter one, What is it like to be a person learning something? Learners, as we encounter them in the classroom, at the reference desk, or in the online environment, are not empty vessels, but individuals who bring an entire personal history, unique background, and distinctively human motivational and cognitive capacities to everything they do. So, when reflecting on this question through the lens of motivation, we need to engage deeply with the psychological research about what makes human beings want to do something and then incorporate that answer into our learner-centered pedagogical strategies.

One way we can consider what it's like to be a person learning something is to investigate what a learner *wants*, from a motivational perspective. What does the evidence tell us about what it's like (or not) to be a motivated person? And how can we apply this understanding to teaching methods that librarians can employ to better facilitate learning?

A key answer to these questions comes from leading educational psychologist and motivational researcher Edward Deci, who writes in his recent book *Why We Do What We Do* that "where the actions of students emanate from their true sense of self, so they are being authentic . . . [we should expect students to] embrace the activity with a sense of interest and commitment."[1] If we break down this statement, we find a general answer to a major question about human motivation. According to Deci, there is a fundamental human desire for authenticity—to be one's true self—and when human beings are given the freedom to express who they really are in their daily activities, their motivation increases.

Though it remains highly influential in the current empirical research on motivation, this view is nothing new. The concept of authenticity and its emphasis on the psychological importance of the expression of the true self have been around about for as long as thinkers have inquired into the nature of being human. At least as far back as Aristotle, we see thinkers positing a correlation between being one's true self and increased meaning in life. The Aristotelian conception of *eudaimonia*—a happy, well-lived, flourishing human life—situates authenticity at its core and involves individuals consistently structuring their lives around performing activities that reflect their true calling. Within this concept neither wealth nor status, pleasure nor fame were the ultimate ends of life. Rather, for Greek moralists such as Aristotle, authenticity was the primary aim of life, and if a person consistently was his true self, other goods like happiness and pleasure would likely follow.[2]

Centuries later, many philosophers after Aristotle, though often possessing fundamentally different worldviews, agreed with the core conclusion that human meaning involved exercising the true self in one's daily activities. Nineteenth-century philosophers Søren Kierkegaard and Friedrich Nietzsche couldn't have been more at odds when it came to their religious views, but they nevertheless agreed that one should live authentically in accordance with one's own values—rather than those of "the crowd" or "herd." As twentieth-century existential psychologist Rollo May puts it, the "central psychological endeavor of Kierkegaard may be summed up under the heading of the question he pursued relentlessly: 'How can you become an individual?'"[3] Interestingly, it was Kierkegaard's thinking that provided the philosophical basis for Carl Rogers's shift away from the Freudian psychoanalysts' "expert-centered" thinking about human meaning and toward a person-centered approach where *who we are as people matters*. As Rogers describes it, "The best way I can state this aim of life, as I see it coming to light in my relationship with my clients, is to use the words of Søren Kierkegaard—'to be that self which one truly is.'"[4] Thus, for the Rogerian humanist, diagnosing an individual is much less productive than facilitating a relationship that provides a safe psychological climate in which a client's true self is free to emerge.

The idea that to be one's true self is an (or *the*) "aim of life" is, to be sure, a bold philosophical hypothesis, as would be any claim of such scope. Nevertheless, it has significant empirical support from the contemporary psychological literature. Rollo May cites Kierkegaard's analysis of the fundamental cause of human despair—an individual's failure to establish authentic selfhood due to conforming to the external expectations of "the crowd"—as revolutionary in its importance for the development of Western psychology generally, and humanistic and existential psychology specifically. There is now a major body of contemporary empirical research in counseling psychology supporting this humanistic-existential (and Kierkegaardian) assumption about the central psychological importance of the true self to human well-being and meaning. Richard Ryan and Edward Deci summarize this research in a 2004 article, writing that "a common theme in the clinical literature is that psychological ill-health is the all too typical product of alienation from one's true self."[5] Essentially, this research shows that people become unhappy when they feel like they are not living lives in accordance with their authentic selves. This evidence supports the hypothesis that being oneself is an integral component of the healthy and well-adjusted human personality.

Interestingly, the centrality of authenticity to human psychology extends beyond Western conceptions of the self and can be seen in a variety of religious and psychological traditions across cultures. For example, the true-self concept plays a significant role in Eastern philosophy, where the *Bhagavad Gita*, the sacred ancient Hindu text, presents the path of Karma Yoga as one of four possible routes to religious enlightenment. Within Hindu religious philosophy, Karma Yoga is one of four ways toward spiritual liberation, one that advocates "selfless service" to others by engaging in authentic individual actions. Though it may seem paradoxical that the way to do good for others is to devote one's life to one's own authentic personal desires—especially within the context of a religious tradition where the dissolution of the ego and one's individual self is of the highest spiritual importance—the *Gita* stresses that practical expressions of the true self can often be the best way to serve others. "The only requirement," religious scholar Patrick S. Bresnan writes on the topic, "is that it be of some genuine value to the community and that, all in all, the person loves the work. This is essential because it is only love that dissolves the grip of ego. If one does not love the work, then it becomes merely a means to an end."[6] Thus, on the path of Karma Yoga, following one's passion is the "path of right action" to selfless service: whenever we do create something out of love, whether it's paint a painting, bake some cookies, or do research that interests us, our actions are selfless.

It is striking that the core ideas of Karma Yoga—the dissolution of one's ego-self by means of the performance of a loved activity—are central to the flow psychology concept discussed by researchers in the growing field of positive psychology. Flow—a psychological state often compared to being "in the zone"—involves being so totally absorbed in what one is currently doing that one ceases to think about oneself in the process. Flow involves a state of "just doing" rather than thinking, which psychologists describe as a peak kind of human experience arising from the pure enjoyment of and engagement with what one is doing.[7]

Thus, Deci's view about the connection between authenticity and motivation follows a historically far-reaching and intellectually diverse tradition in thinking about human meaning, one that continues to the present day. In a 2009 article psychologist Rebecca Schlegel and her colleagues described finding that during activities when individuals felt their true self to be present, they experienced the activity as more meaningful than activities during which they felt their authentic self to be missing. And activities that were deemed to be meaningful were highly motivating: as human beings, we *want* to do things we find meaningful.[8]

This research provides a psychological foundation for understanding why significant learning is more meaningful and lasting than learning without self-motivation. Significant learning involves knowledge that has existential significance (that is, personal meaning to the learner), so it follows that we're much more inclined as learners to want to engage with such material. Kevin *wants* to remember where the New Beverly Cinema is on Beverly Boulevard in Los Angeles because it's his favorite place to watch movies, but he'll probably never remember where his neighbor's special effects studio is in Burbank since he has no significant personal investment in going there. The true-self connection not only motivates us, but also helps make learning stick.

Before moving on to more explicitly explore the connection between authenticity and learning, we want to say something about the nature of authenticity and the true self. As we discussed in the introduction, though the ideas in this book may have an origin in philosophy or psychology, we do not ultimately find any value in such ideas unless they are both empirically supported *and* applicable in a practical way. While notions of the true self may sound like highfalutin concepts belonging to the realm of platonic ideas, which might be difficult to deliver on in library (or any other empirical) reality, we don't feel that this needs to be the case. For example, authenticity is a highly measurable, definable concept that has been treated as an operational variable in many recent empirical studies.

Following this research, we understand authenticity as "the unobstructed operation of one's true, or core, self in one's daily enterprise."[9] And, by true self, we don't mean anything essentialist or New-Agey. We understand the true self, following on the literature, as "the aspects of the self that are considered by the person to represent who they really are."[10] This concept of true self allows the self to be iterative and in a process of constant change and takes the individual's feelings of meaning as the ultimate measure of authentic behavior. We would consider a particular task to be an authentic representation of the true self for a person if *she* felt it was meaningful and reflected the core of what she wanted to be doing. For example, this condition would obtain for Kevin if he were to write an article on authentic learning because it's a matter he cares deeply about and enjoys writing about. But this would not be the case if he were commissioned to write an article designed to convince librarians that some technological gadget was the best way to connect with learners.

Having established this concrete understanding of what it means to have an authentic self and why it is so critical to motivating individuals, we now dive into considering the implications of these ideas for a learner-centered conception of information literacy and related library work.

Authentic Learning: The Primary Goal of the (Information Literacy) Educator

From the psychological research on authenticity comes an answer that fills in the context to our central question of this book—What is it like to be a person learning something? At least from a motivational perspective, it involves a desire to express one's true self within the learning context. The individual learner before us is not a blank slate, but an embodied existential being with a deep desire to express who he is, no matter the context. Our conception of learner-centered pedagogy is centrally informed by this idea. Indeed, our very concept of information literacy, as the set of skills allowing learners to use information to think well about what matters to them (as defined in chapter one), is derived from the core psychological idea that authenticity is at the heart of human motivation and desire. But still we might wonder: Why does authenticity need to be *so* central to information literacy education, and why do we think it's so essentially tied up with learning for the learner-centered teacher-librarian?

You can now see that our definition of information literacy is strongly informed by the research on authenticity and motivation. Additionally, the same tradition in humanistic psychology led by Carl Rogers also advocated the importance of allowing learners to bring their true selves to their schoolwork. Philosophically inclined psychologists as far back as John Dewey "stressed the importance of engaging children in projects that interested them, both as a foundation to meaningful learning and as a way to develop responsible members of society."[11] This served as the basis for the Rogerian conception of significant learning, which you may recall involves the retention and transfer of ideas that are personally significant *to the learner.* More importantly, Rogers's claims have been borne out by contemporary research in educational psychology, which draws the connection between authenticity and learning just as strongly and brings empirical evidence along for support.

A leading contemporary textbook in educational psychology confirms Rogers's sense of the importance of significant learning, noting that the "interest students show in an activity or in an area of knowledge predicts how much they will attend to it and how well they process, comprehend, and remember it," which hits on each element of our concept of learning as defined in the previous chapter.[12] Similarly, in a recent article, researchers Assor, Kaplan, and Roth go so far to say,

> The primary task of the teacher is to try to understand their students' authentic interests and goals, and then help students to understand the connection between their personal goals and interests and schoolwork. In addition, teachers may also find or develop tasks that fit their students' interests. When students do not have clear personal interests and goals, teachers may assist them in developing such interests and goals.[13]

This is a particularly striking passage, as it situates the facilitation of authentic learning as the central task—rather than simply *a* task—of the learner-centered educator. Furthermore, it gives concrete suggestions for precisely how such authentic learning can be facilitated: educators can spend their time getting to know their learners as individuals—*who they are as people matters*—and with this knowledge in place, help learners tie their true selves to the preexisting educational curriculum.

When we apply this understanding to the information literacy context, we see that helping learners locate, interpret, evaluate, and use information that matters to them is the central goal of information literacy education precisely because this is a fundamental goal of education itself.[14] A library educator's specific contribution to this general goal, as Rogers implied many years ago, may be resource based. But it won't *only* be resource based. A key nuance for learner-centered librarians is that they provide resources to learners *to the extent that these resources connect in a meaningful way to a learner's true self.*

One important implication of this view is that the librarian who provides resources that do not align with a learner's true self—even if they are good or reliable sources—is not engaged in a learner-centered teaching practice. For example, if a student came to the reference desk looking for information on Spanish poetry and Dani connected him with resources on Renaissance Spanish poetry, but the student was actually interested in contemporary Latino spoken word, then she would not have accomplished her learner-centered goal. If nothing else, the research that we've discussed so far tells us that learner-centered librarians must believe that *who our learners are as people matters* and must therefore view the goal of all their pedagogical activities to be contributing directly to significant learning.

We return to this central learner-centered ethos of librarianship throughout the rest of this book, examining it through a variety of lenses. Beginning in the next section, we discuss concrete approaches, at both the macro and micro levels, for facilitating authentic learning within the information literacy context.

Authenticity in Action:
Applications to the Information Literacy Context

Any of the pedagogical ideas in this book can be implemented at both macro and micro levels within librarianship, ranging from broad-scale information literacy outreach initiatives to working with an individual learner at the reference desk. Working toward operationalizing significant learning—where research involves the direct expression of a learner's true self—is no different, and in this section we explore specific examples of how this learner-centered idea can be incorporated into library practice at every level of our work. Of course, this will (and should!) look different for librarians at different institutions since each library has its own context. However, one enormous advantage of the learner-centered approach is that the general framework of authentic learning is highly adaptable, and therefore transferable, no matter where one works. Consequently, the examples we supply in this section are by no means a rulebook for how learner-centered strategies should be applied in your library (though you're more than welcome and encouraged to borrow them!). Through these examples we hope to inspire reflection on how you might use your librarian expertise to transfer similar strategies—and use your creativity to come up with new applications—to your own work as an information literacy educator.

At all levels, the learner-centered librarian is fundamentally concerned with advocating that research is about significant learning and that the librarian's primary role is to help learners use information in ways that allow them to bring their true selves to their work. At the macro level in an academic library, the concept of authentic learning can be a fundamental driving force behind coordinating an information literacy program, both in terms of collaborating with other individual instructors on campus and advocating for the library's central place in student learning. Authentic learning can be the cornerstone for building any information literacy program, starting with the most fundamental question: What is research? Too often we allow assumptions, whether those of students, faculty members, administrators, or even other librarians (and ourselves!), to determine the answer to this question. But this is problematic since it often results in the exact scenarios that the learner-centered librarian hopes to avoid, where learners simply do the bare minimum necessary to satisfy the demands of their assignments rather than explore research topics they are passionate about.

Indeed, one finding of Kevin's graduate research on authenticity and learning within the information literacy instruction context was that unless learners are given explicit instruction on how to develop authentic research questions, they will almost always choose a topic because they think it will be easy to find information on it, even if the topic does not interest them.[15] Given our preceding discussion about motivation and learning, it won't surprise you that this research also indicated that these students reported learning less than the students who dug a little deeper and chose topics that reflected their authentic interests. Despite having worse outcomes, many students have been conditioned (like eleventh-grade Kevin) to believe there is a major difference between the things they might look up on their own time and the things that qualify as legitimate research topics in the classroom. This is true *even if* instructors encourage students to choose a topic that is interesting to them relative to the class assignment, as learners simply may not see how to bridge the gap between their authentic selves and academic demands.

Kevin experienced a macro-level example of this phenomenon when he was asked, as information literacy coordinator at his former workplace, to hold a workshop for a group of new teaching assistants for a first-year communication course about research. These TAs were tasked with helping students do research for a speech assignment, and the professor in charge of the course wanted Kevin's "expert" advice to help train them (no pressure!).

Situations like this can be challenging: what does one say to a group of graduate students (in front of a faculty colleague, no less) to help them teach students how to do better research? Not only is this situation difficult pedagogically, but Kevin also felt a lot of pressure to succeed. After all, his job was to coordinate information literacy on campus, and the opportunity to speak to and be directly involved in the mentoring of TAs working with almost all first-year students at the university was an enormous opportunity for him, the library's information literacy program, and the library in general.

One potential strategy for this situation is to use the workshop to make sure the TAs have a solid understanding of library research. Students can learn to be better researchers if they know, for example, that liaison librarians are available to help them, which informational resources the library offers, and, of course, how to successfully search the library databases. To guarantee that all undergraduates get this information, it would be wise to make sure that the TAs themselves know these things and to use the training as an opportunity to offer explicit instruction in these matters.

Instead of this more traditional strategy, however, Kevin decided to try something new and focus the training around significant learning. Doing so was a bit scary, as it usually is with trying something new—in the classroom or elsewhere. It can feel safe and comfortable to do the expected thing or what we've always done, and Kevin definitely felt anxiety about doing things differently. What if the TAs just wanted to hear about databases and didn't care about the whole significant learning idea? What if they thought he was weird? What if someone told the dean he was not doing a good job? All these things went through Kevin's head, but he made a conscious choice to proceed in a way that promoted significant learning, knowing that this approach was backed by the research and that he had the best interests of learners in mind. In this and many other cases, remembering that *pedagogy is about learning rather than our teaching* can be extremely helpful for overcoming psychological barriers to trying out ideas that may feel risky at the outset.

Kevin pulled up a few PowerPoint slides with quotes about authentic learning and explained to the TAs how he likes to talk to students about research: he tries to make students understand that research is about pursuing questions that matter to *you* and developing the tools to do that in a way that fits within the formal requirements of your coursework, with the library being a major one of those tools. This was a direct application of this book's definition of information literacy and Assor, Kaplan, and Roth's quote about authentic learning as the primary task of the teacher in this chapter's previous section. Kevin then showed an example of "research as authentic inquiry" relating to his own life and demonstrated how the TAs could apply a similar strategy to their classes' research topic for the semester: issues in higher education.

Kevin's approach to this discussion also was somewhat unusual but directly aligned with the idea that information literacy involves using information to think well about what matters to learners. Students, he said, are often inclined, given an assignment like this, to come up with very "school-sounding" research inquiries that they may lack a significant personal connection to. For example, students in the past had researched things like "higher education policy in California." Though there is nothing inherently wrong with that topic, previous TAs reported a frustrating lack of engagement with these topics. The reason for this, Kevin (silently!) diagnosed, was the learner's lack of meaningful connection with such an abstract topic. Indeed, when students experience a lack of connection to their research, we should *expect* a corresponding lack of motivation.

So Kevin suggested an alternative approach: research could be about authenticity, vulnerability, and the true self just as much as it could be about the broader topic of the development of society-wide policy. Rather than trying to convince students that a topic they've been assigned is important (e.g., "Issues in higher education matter; they affect the foundations of a democratic society!"), the reverse approach could be pursued. Why not begin with the existential realities of students' lives within the context of higher education—the ones that directly connect with the individual self—and then, through this sense of personal connection, relate those ideas to broader societal issues?

To demonstrate this alternative based on significant learning, Kevin used the following examples. Many students new to the university may be experiencing loneliness or homesickness or depression since they are gone from home and solely responsible for themselves for the first time. Some may be unaccustomed to constant dining hall food and struggle with their weight and lack of healthy food options (consider the dreaded "freshman 15"). Some students may feel peer pressure to fit in by partying and drinking, despite not especially enjoying these activities on a constant basis, because they don't know how to connect without participating in them. Many may be the first member of their family to go to college and struggle seeing themselves in the higher education system. Many students grapple with issues of existential meaning at this stage of their lives since they are making major life decisions—by choosing a major and investigating potential career options—and have difficulty determining who they want to be. Others may just not be able to stand their roommates and could perhaps use their research to explore empirically validated communication strategies to help them through this trying situation.

Kevin stressed that, from the standpoint of authentic learning, all of these issues—or ones like them—are valid avenues of research. To demonstrate this, Kevin brainstormed different research concepts a student would need to explore to satisfactorily investigate questions based on these issues. Guiding a student in formulating keywords related to these questions and then using the library (or Google) to find reliable information on them is something completely familiar to librarians and within the usual purview of their expertise. But the main learner-centered twist on the proceedings was to situate these information literacy skills within the context of significant learning. We would still discuss things like keywords, databases, and how librarians could help these beginning students; however, we're only interested in discussing these issues to the extent that these resources, ideas, and skills connect in a meaningful way to the students' true selves. Providing this context not only gave the TAs a new way to place these particular research skills (most of which they were already aware) into a meaningful, learner-centered context, but also demonstrated the substantial contribution that librarians can have on learning beyond providing students with resources: They can be legitimate partners in facilitating significant learning.

After the session, Kevin e-mailed the instructor responsible for the TAs to thank her for the session and let her know what wonderful collaborators the TAs had been. He received the following reply:

> We thought YOU were wonderful! We loved your examples! You have such a great way of relating to students and are so student-centered. You really demystify research. Thanks so much!
>
> By the way, I ended up using the Freshman 15 idea in the big lecture and it worked out really well.

We find it particularly interesting that even though Kevin never used the words *learner-centered* or *student-centered* during the workshop, this is exactly what came across to another educator when significant learning, authenticity, and how to implement them within the context of research, were the core elements of the session. Merely suggesting that topics like disliking one's roommate could be a perfectly valid source of scholarly research and, critically, modeling how that could work, was a major pedagogical breakthrough.

This is just one of many examples in our work where we've seen that an approach based on significant learning had the potential not only to change learners' attitudes toward research, but also to radically alter the role of librarians within the university context. In this situation, it was clear that, though the professor and TAs had encouraged their students in the past to pursue their interests, they were not entirely sure how to implement the pedagogical practices that would facilitate this kind of significant learning in practice. And really, why would they be? After all, they're experts in their subject matter and not necessarily in the finer pedagogical details relating to information literacy and motivation. This is one place where learner-centered librarians—educators with a solid grounding in the theory and practice of learner-centered pedagogy, but not necessarily steeped in the disciplinary norms of the given course—can truly shine and bring additional value to the classroom.

Indeed, modeling strategies for developing what we might call "authentic topics"—research inquiries and questions based on a learner's true sense of self—is an excellent, practically oriented way librarians can put significant learning into action at the macro level. A whole information literacy program can be built around the idea that research involves significant learning. Consequently, the learner-centered reference and instruction librarian's time can be spent reflecting on, designing, and implementing strategies that learners can use to develop authentic topics. For example, at one library he worked at, Kevin created a series of online modules that broke down the step-by-step process of developing a research question. The module on "developing a research topic that interests you" began with a sample assignment and then walked students through a thinking process where they'd develop a topic of personal interest that met the requirements of their assignment. To support this, Dani created a flowchart handout designed to help students walk through choosing a topic, based on the ideas of authenticity and significant learning that we've discussed in this chapter (figure 2.1).

This worksheet is just one way of helping students identify a topic that is meaningful to them, but we've included it here as an example of the type of language one might use to talk about significant learning and to demonstrate that it is completely possible to engage with these ideas outside a face-to-face classroom or reference desk interaction (even though these tools can be helpful in those scenarios as well!).

Along with the module on developing a research topic, Kevin also created ones on developing keywords, evaluating sources, and other topics that are typically covered in an introductory library session. What makes these modules unique, though, is the central focus on research as an expression of the true self. Even those modules that didn't obviously lend themselves to this idea, such as evaluating information, were connected to the idea of significant learning.

Beyond helping individual students navigate the research process, the modules served an important macro-level function for Kevin. They gave him something concrete to point to when he advocated the value of information literacy to campus stakeholders. It's one thing to say, "I really care about students being engaged with research, and I think I can help your students be motivated to learn," and quite another to be able to show someone the specific pedagogical strategies you use to carry off that learner-centered approach. Creating these modules led to a variety of opportunities to collaborate with other campus partners. For example, Kevin went to the university learning center, which offers tutoring and writing assistance for students, to discuss the potential for collaboration. Kevin outlined his approach to research as authentic inquiry and was immediately asked if he'd be willing to give a workshop on this subject in the learning center. He eventually trained all learning center writing tutors in the learner-centered approach and even held research tutoring hours in the learning center itself. It was a great way to reach many students on campus who might not otherwise have used the library or understood what librarians did, and it all started by sharing the ideas about significant learning outlined in this chapter.

FIGURE 2.1 **TOPIC SELECTION FLOWCHART**

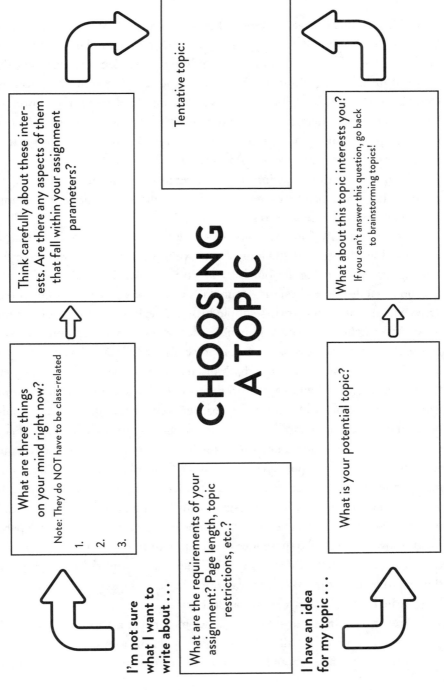

CHOOSING A TOPIC

I'm not sure what I want to write about . . .

What are the requirements of your assignment? Page length, topic restrictions, etc.?

What are three things on your mind right now?
Note: They do NOT have to be class-related

1.

2.

3.

Think carefully about these interests. Are there any aspects of them that fall within your assignment parameters?

Tentative topic:

What about this topic interests you?
If you can't answer this question, go back to brainstorming topics!

What is your potential topic?

I have an idea for my topic . . .

And here's the fascinating thing: when Kevin recently started a new job in a totally different context, he ended up initiating a very similar collaboration he'd had at his previous institution, simply by offhandedly mentioning the idea of "authentic learning" to the head of the learning center on his new campus. These kinds of incidents have demonstrated to us the power of learner-centered pedagogy as we've defined it in this book and have helped us develop the confidence to apply these principles to our work without reservation. Our experience advocating these ideas indicates there's something about significant learning that transcends one institutional context or another. It's a *human* phenomenon. When we discuss significant learning, people take notice because it resonates on a deep level.

Now, we certainly don't want you to simply take our word for it. We know that you'll be able to find all kinds of creative ways to advocate and incorporate significant learning at your own institutions. Maybe you're really into instructional design and can use your skills to create a super-awesome interactive video that blows Kevin's simple little PowerPoint modules out of the water and catches fire with a bunch of professors on your campus or even across the library profession after you present it at LOEX. Maybe you're on a general education committee that's discussing a redesign of the first-year writing program and you happen to mention that you think you have some very effective, empirically informed learner-centered strategies that would be perfect for engaging students with research early in their undergraduate careers. Or maybe you've been looking for a practical way to move your reference and instruction department away from old-school bibliographic instruction toward a more conceptually based, learner-centered approach, and an honest conversation about significant learning can help you create a dialogue with your colleagues about possible new directions for your department. However you take these ideas and run with them, we're excited to see the creative ways that librarians employ ideas about significant learning at the macro level in their own libraries and the deep impact they can have on large-scale learning initiatives in the process.

However, let's bring things back down to earth for a moment. Though large-scale initiatives are all well and good, we know that much of our day-to-day work as reference and instruction librarians takes place at a micro level, teaching individual classes, leading workshops, or working with learners one-on-one at the reference desk. It's here, really, that we can see significant learning happening in its purest form, when we have the chance to work with learners to directly develop authentic topics within the context of their schoolwork.

While writing this chapter, Kevin was working at the reference desk when a question came through the chat reference service that almost perfectly illustrates what it means to implement the concept of significant learning at the micro level.

The question was a general one. A student had an assignment that required her to use Academic Search Premier to search for articles on her topic, and she needed help locating the database through the library's home page. This scenario is probably very familiar to anyone who has spent time on a reference desk, and that's why we like it so much. At first glance, it's not obvious how we might incorporate super-lofty ideas like "expression of the true self and significant learning" in day-to-day work at the reference desk. But, typical of many reference questions, as the conversation continued the opportunities to take the student further than just locating a database became clear.

Indeed, after helping the student access Academic Search Premier, which took some time and patience at the student's pace, it seemed like the interaction was wrapping up. And the student seemed pretty much done with the conversation, though it's well documented that those cues can be much harder to discern in the online environment than in person at the desk. Just to check, Kevin asked the student if she would like help searching Academic Search Premier or any other resource for articles on her topic. The student quickly agreed ("Yes!") and explained that her topic was phobias.

At that moment, Kevin is fully willing to admit, his knee-jerk response was far from learner-centered and more along the lines of, Oh man, how am I supposed to type *phobia* into Academic Search Premier and help this student get anything remotely useful for her research?! The problem, of course, is that *phobia* is too broad a term to serve as the foundation for a meaningful research problem query. As any librarian knows, a key part of preparing to conduct a search within the information literacy context involves helping learners find a topic that is the appropriate size for beginning their search (not too broad, not too narrow, Goldilocks style), and *phobia* just wasn't going to cut it.

One way to handle this situation is to say something like, "Okay, we'll need to narrow this down a bit since 'phobia' is pretty broad. Is there something more specific you'd like to focus on?" Kevin actually did ask this, and the student responded, "No, not really, my professor just said it had to be about phobias." So, keeping the concept of significant learning forefront in his mind, Kevin thought to himself, Is there some way that I can help the student narrow down her topic by connecting it to herself so that it becomes significant for her?

After a brief pause, Kevin typed the following into the reference chat box: "'Phobias' is pretty general, so I think a good strategy might be to pick something that interests you about phobias. For example, do you have any phobias? Like, I'm afraid of flying, so I might look up 'fear of flying.' Do you know what I mean?"

Even though the interaction was through chat and therefore somewhat impersonal and anonymous, Kevin thought, he could still invite the student to reflect on her personal relationship to phobias and even model (however briefly) for her the kind of vulnerability he was talking about by sharing an example of a real phobia of his own.

The student replied that she did understand—actually, she was arachnophobic—and "definitely wouldn't mind" doing some research on her fear of spiders. In a traditional reference interaction, it would have been entirely expected and appropriate for Kevin to remain on the surface of this question and talk to the student in a general way about narrowing down her research question. But by throwing in a quick personal line, in the hopes of facilitating a learning experience where the student reflected on her own nature, Kevin successfully pointed the research in a personally significant direction for her.

Research about spiders may not, on the surface, be a groundbreaking example of learner-centered pedagogy, but these topics need to be personally relevant, not earth-shattering or mind-blowing. This learning experience, however small, helped that student connect her authentic self to her schoolwork and subsequently helped her break down the topic so she could find information on it. Ultimately, she used information to think well about something that mattered to her, which is the whole point of significant information-literacy learning.

Finally, Kevin stressed that the student could use a similar strategy for any future research assignment, no matter the topic. What they'd just done together was work on a skill that *transfers:* any time she had a research project, she could reflect on herself in relation to that project and develop a research question that let her explore her interests within the constraints of the assignment. And because that can be tricky and take lots of practice, Kevin pointed out that, when looking to brainstorm a topic that interests her, talking to a librarian about finding a topic is always a good strategy.

When the student thanked Kevin at the end of the chat for being "really helpful," it meant something more to him than normal. He felt good for having helped a student engage deeply with her schoolwork, when all too often learners can feel alienated from it. In the learner-centered model, we know that *who we are as people matters*, and even in this brief interaction he'd helped a learner explore something that directly bore on who she was as a person—something that made her afraid and evidence-based solutions for overcoming that fear. It was significant learning in action, right there within the context of an ordinary chat session on a typical day working at the reference desk.

You may have noticed that in all these examples, macro and micro, we bring the concept of significant learning into the equation at the topic-development stage of the research process. We think this is the most helpful place for librarians to interject authentic topics into the equation, when possible, since this is the make-or-break spot when students develop a query, which can either reflect their true self or not. If this stage goes awry and, for whatever reason, the student chooses a topic that doesn't reflect his authentic self, the rest of his research may be affected, and his motivation (and, subsequently, learning) will almost certainly decrease.

This is why you'll find both of us, in our own reference and instructional activities, focusing so much energy on the pre-search/topic-development stage of the research process and offering multiple examples throughout this book for how to break down this stage of research. Since everything else follows from this moment, we think it's the key for setting up a significant learning interaction in the library context.

Authenticity Involves More than Just Interests: The Importance of Autonomy over Control

In this chapter so far we've thought about how an individual's desire to express her authentic self is a central consideration for learning, and for inspiring a person to *want* to learn something, or what we call motivation. But this is just one piece of the motivational puzzle. Several other elements besides a person's interests go into motivating someone to learn (or not).

One reason we stress that motivation is about more than just learners' interests—for example, having them write about tennis if they like tennis, or even deeper existential issues they may be experiencing—is that there is a practical danger of turning our understanding of the connection between authenticity and motivation into something of a gimmick. If the takeaway from this chapter were simply that we think learners' interests are important, for example, we would be failing to see that involving students' interests in the classroom is just one practical way out of many to address a deep psychological fact about human behavior. In fact, we've seen this in action when a librarian suggests "telling students to write about something that interests them" as a reference or instructional strategy, rather than thinking about it as a manifestation of the understanding that *who we are as people matters* for learning. We think this difference matters a great deal because it can have practical implications for a learner's motivation. But what's the difference between a librarian who approaches developing learners' interests as a mere strategy and one who does so in a deeply learner-centered way?

To answer this question, we need to introduce an important distinction between two types of motivation: intrinsic and extrinsic. Individuals are *intrinsically motivated* when they pursue an activity purely for its own sake, for the love of the activity itself (recall our discussion of Karma Yoga earlier in the chapter). These are *autonomously chosen* behaviors: they are done with a sense of freedom, individuality, and personal choice because the individual wants to do them. In short, intrinsically motivated behaviors involve free expression of the true self. We see this sense of intrinsically motivated self-governance in actions as wide ranging as going to a Dodgers game because you love baseball, writing a short story because you have something you need to get off your chest, or making some cupcakes because you love to bake. And of course we also see intrinsic motivation in action when we engage in a research project whose impetus comes from grappling with a question that matters deeply to us, even if the larger project itself was originally assigned to us.

The common element among all these behaviors, on one level, is that the individual likes them. However, from the standpoint of intrinsic motivation, the important element is not merely that one likes doing them—in fact, sometimes these activities can be kind of unpleasant in some ways. After all, the drive down Sunset into Dodger Stadium can be less than ideal if you're stuck in traffic trying to get on the 101 freeway, writing a short story can be awfully hard and lonely, and sometimes you burn your hand while trying to get the cupcakes of your dreams out of the oven. No, at a deeper level, these activities all involve free, autonomous choice: the ability to determine your own life as you see fit.

In contrast, whereas intrinsic motivation involves a sense of autonomy and authenticity, extrinsically motivated behaviors involve a sense of external control. Let's define *extrinsic motivation* as behaviors done solely to satisfy an authority other than ourselves. In this sense, unlike autonomous behavior where individuals are the authors of their actions, extrinsically motivated behavior is controlled by external demands. Imagine that, instead of going to the game because you love the Dodgers, you must attend to impress a client coming from out of town who has insisted on going to see Dodger Stadium. You feel forced to go, which feels a whole lot different than if you attended solely because you love the game. Similarly, it would not surprise motivational researchers if you procrastinated on that short story you had to write for your senior-year English class, when all you wanted to do was be out with your friends. Actions that are controlled from the outside are generally less meaningful to the individual; therefore, externally controlled activities are, from a motivational perspective, far less engaging than those that come from within.

Now we can understand that our central, learner-centered question, What is it like to be a person learning something? involves a desire to express our true selves—in terms of our interests, curiosities, passions, and struggles—*and* to engage in learning in an autonomy-supportive rather than controlling environment. This broader understanding of motivation can help us avoid turning something like discovering learners' interests into a simple gimmick falling under the learner-centered heading. A learner's interests and curiosities fundamentally matter, but if we encourage learners to pursue their interests in a controlling environment, their motivation will almost certainly be undermined. It is therefore a matter of enormous pedagogical importance that we understand how we can, as information literacy educators, avoid controlling our learners.

Of course, this is easier said than done. Any educational situation that doesn't immediately devolve into chaos necessarily involves at least some sense of control over learners. For example, we need basic classroom rules to provide a safe and productive learning environment. And, at a more conceptual level, all good educators have a planned curriculum with concrete learning objectives for students to achieve. But particular outcomes of this curriculum may not necessarily line up with learners' autonomous desires for what they wanted to do that day and how they wanted to do it. When this is the case, how do we reconcile the human desire for self-direction with the educator's need to assert some level of control over learners? Are learner-centered strategies possible in a world that demands some conformity from the individual for society to function productively?

No surprise here: we do think it's possible to satisfy the need for pedagogical structure without undermining learner autonomy. And empathy is the most powerful tool the learner-centered educator can use to facilitate significant learning. Our ability to put ourselves in our learners' shoes, adopt their perspectives as autonomous agents, and adjust our pedagogical practices accordingly allows us to create a learning environment that privileges autonomy over control while still allowing educators to meet their learning goals. Indeed, educational psychologist Johnmarshall Reeve has noted that perhaps the most important thing a learner-centered educator can do to begin supporting learners' autonomy is simply to recognize the elements of a controlling style, and make a conscious effort to be more autonomy supportive.[16] For this reason, it's important to understand the core psychological elements at play in each of these motivational styles.

In a controlling learning environment, only the educator's perspective matters. We suspect that this was the central problem with the motivational style employed by the eleventh-grade English teacher in the example at the beginning of this chapter. When a learner's perspective is not given *any* credence in determining his own learning, the relationship between teacher and learner becomes an adversarial one because it poses a fundamental threat to the learner's autonomy. In the most extreme sense, the adversarial educator might think something like, Well I just don't care what the students *want* to learn about or *how* they want to learn it or any of this touchy-feely learner-centered garbage. This isn't about them and what they want to do. I've got a curriculum—the stuff these kids *should* know—and I'm going to teach it to them!

Though this may seem like an extreme position, we've both seen and experienced quite a few educators, including librarians, adopt something like this in practice without even being aware of it. We run the risk of being controlling whenever we fail to ask ourselves, What is it like to be a person learning something? Indeed, what seems to be fundamentally missing from the controlling motivation style is any sense at all that *who our learners are as people matters*. Since no attempt to understand the learner's perspective has been made, one way to characterize the controlling style is that it occurs when educators fail to make *empathy* central to their pedagogical practice. Given what we understand about motivation, it's no wonder that learners would strongly resist this approach.

Putting this all together, we can understand an empathic motivating style to be one that understands that *learners want to express their true selves in an environment that involves as little control as possible*. This does not mean, however, that we must go to the opposite extreme and think that only the learner's perspective matters. An autonomy-supportive style instead reaches a middle ground, recognizing that *both perspectives*, those of the learner and the facilitator of learning, matter. Rather than an adversarial relationship, where the perspectives of the educator and learner are fundamentally opposed, we find it helpful to imagine the autonomy-supportive style as involving a more nuanced *relationship dialectic* between learner and facilitator, where empathy serves as the bridge toward significant learning. In this picture, a reconciliation where a teacher nurtures a learner's innate sense of motivation while also meeting curricular learning outcomes *is* possible.

We finish this chapter by fleshing out the empathic elements of the autonomy-supportive style through considering some practical applications drawn from the empirical literature in educational psychology as well as some ways we can adapt these ideas to the information literacy context.

Supporting Autonomy in Practice

In a recent meta-analysis of the research on the autonomy-supportive versus controlling motivation style, Reeve outlines the significant benefits that learners attain by having access to autonomy-supportive educators.[17] Compared to those exposed primarily to the controlling style, learners in an autonomy-supportive environment exhibit increased motivational outcomes such as intrinsic motivation, curiosity, and creativity; increased psychological outcomes such as self-esteem, self-worth, and overall psychological well-being; education-related outcomes such as deeper conceptual understanding, higher grades, and better standardized test scores; and better feelings toward their educational experience as measured by increased identification with school, persistence through difficulty, and decreased dropout rates. It's one heck of an impressive list, touching on just about every cognitive, emotional, and psychological dimension involved in the process of learning.

Nevertheless, the research also indicates that, even with such profound benefits for our learners, the natural tendency of many educators is to fall back into a controlling style. As Rogers (and even Freud) noted many years ago, society values control and external demands over free individual expression, and this tends to transfer over to the classroom context, even among the best-intentioned educators. This may lead to a tendency to equate a structured learning environment (which we *do* need, to some extent) with a controlling one. However, given the overwhelming evidence against the controlling style, we are now confident that a structured learning environment that affords learners significant freedom to express themselves in a manner they find freeing is possible.

Reeve offers five concrete strategies for how educators can be more autonomy supportive in the classroom:

1. nurture learners' inner motivational resources
2. provide explanatory rationales
3. use informal, noncontrolling language and behaviors
4. display the patience required to allow learners to work at their own pace
5. acknowledge learners' negative affect.[18]

We outline each of these applications in turn and, in each scenario, consider examples of how these principles can apply to our work as information literacy educators.

1. NURTURE LEARNERS' INNER MOTIVATIONAL RESOURCES

When we nurture a learner's inner motivational resources, we view our learner as a whole person, with a deep inner drive for authentic self-expression. We consider our learners' interests, passions, and personal life goals and strive to help them tie these goals to a preexisting curriculum, rather than dismissing these interests or goals as not worthy of our attention or as merely getting in the way of the curriculum we're trying to follow. We establish that school is a place for who they are, not who we would like them to be. Though we've considered (and will continue to consider) many examples of this idea in action so far, one more example comes to mind that we think expands on the autonomy-supportive elements of this idea.

Several years ago, Kevin was working late one night at the main research library at UNC, when a student approached him with a unique request. The student was looking to start an anarchist campus political group, and he'd been instructed that, to be officially recognized, the group must reflect a serious intellectual endeavor that was relevant to the campus. Perhaps it's not altogether surprising that the idea of a university-sponsored political group advocating anarchy—commonly understood to involve lawlessness and destruction—might have seemed a little questionable to a major research university. So, this need brought the student to the reference desk, where he asked Kevin if he knew of anywhere on campus that might be able to help him establish anarchism as credible.

Rather than referring the student elsewhere, Kevin's response was, "Yeah, how about the library?" Kevin explained that, at least in his opinion, one way to show its legitimacy might be to document that anarchism, as a political philosophy, has a serious intellectual tradition and history. Kevin and the student then went to the library catalog and found several books on anarchism that the library owned. Kevin pointed out that this would be yet another argument that anarchism was a legitimate political topic at the university: UNC's own library holds tons of books on the subject! Sometime later, the student approached Kevin again at the reference desk and let him know that the group had been approved; since 2012 an anarchist group called the UNControllables have been an official part of student life at the university.

Now we don't mention this example to make fun of the fact that UNC was skeptical of an anarchist group or to suggest that the university shouldn't make groups justify their intellectual foundations in order to become an officially recognized campus entity. In fact, it's the exact opposite. We think the administration's policy was actually *very* autonomy supportive, precisely because the student wasn't simply dismissed out of hand. By affording the students an opportunity to use reason, argument, and research to explain their case, campus administration effectively said, "Look, you're more than welcome to make the case that this is a campus issue, and we're more than willing to listen if you'd like to take the steps to make an argument for why this group should exist."

Here we see a direct application of a *relationship dialectic based in empathy* that respects both learner and educator: We (the university) are happy to listen to your (an anarchist group's) perspective if you listen to our perspective (the need to have student groups grounded in intellectual rationales). This is in direct contrast to Kevin's teacher who was not willing to listen to his perspective on Johnny Rotten, in spite of the enormous body of scholarly literature that exists on his importance as a historical figure, which ultimately resulted in an adversarial situation that not only decreased Kevin's motivation, but implicitly led him to internalize the sense that school was not a place where who he was as a person mattered.

One other element of Kevin's interaction at the reference desk worth remarking on is that it follows directly from the Rogerian conception of significant learning, where a facilitator of learning helped a student break down an intellectual problem and then provided resources that matched his goals and interests. Probably like any other average student, the founder of the anarchist group did not see that the library could help solve this problem, but Kevin was able to use his subject knowledge and informational expertise to help the student locate something significant to his life. This was an unexpected opportunity to nurture a student's inner motivational resources, but Kevin was prepared to deal with it by keeping the idea of autonomy-supportive teaching in mind. And when even an anarchist can recognize that their university is a place for him, you know that autonomy-supportive approaches must be on to something!

And though this particular example involved an empathic dialectic between the institution and the student, as well as Kevin and the student, there will be many reference and instruction interactions where the librarian can serve as a kind of autonomy-supportive conduit in what may otherwise end up being a controlling relationship between a professor and learner, had the librarian not intervened. This can be the case even in situations where a professor may have the absolute best intentions, as in the case of the class that we discussed earlier where students were tasked to write about issues in higher education. Until a librarian intervened and modeled how to nurture learners' inner motivational resources, the students' default setting was to please an external authority—their professor—by choosing a topic that "seemed scholarly." This is what we like to call a sneakily controlling situation: It doesn't seem controlling at all—in fact, both the professor and TAs *wanted* to engage their students in the subject matter—but if you examine the situation in more detail, you very clearly see a learning environment predicated more on external than intrinsic motivation. This is what the research means by *control*, and given the extensive evidence against this kind of motivating style, we want to be extremely mindful of situations where controlling elements driven by external demands may be lurking beneath the surface.

And these elements may be present more often than we're inclined to think. As reference and instruction librarians, we often recognize that a learner's initial query may not be what they're actually asking; therefore, a good reference interview will usually involve digging deeper into a learner's question: "Oh, you asked for a book on Joni Mitchell, but if we inquire just a little more we can help you develop your research question on the Laurel Canyon music scene in the 1970s" (which perhaps is the broader question that the learner was interested in). Similarly, as autonomy-supportive librarians aimed toward significant learning, we now know to never take a learner's question at face value *from the standpoint of intrinsic motivation*. Instead of asking ourselves, Is this the information the learner really needs to answer her information need? we can take a step back and ask, Is this a question that actually matters to the learner? We might end up asking more or less the same follow-up questions, but it comes from a very different place, one more autonomy supportive than the other. The evidence speaks for itself about which environment is more conducive to learning.

2. PROVIDE EXPLANATORY RATIONALES

We noted earlier a paradox between autonomy and control related to learning—intrinsic motivation seems to require absolute freedom, but a structured learning environment will always limit learners' autonomy, at least in some ways. Think about this in the simplest terms related to libraries. How many students seem *excited* to come to the library for an instruction session? Dani will admit to skipping out on library day in her first-year humanities class, preferring to take a nap that day. I already know how to find books and articles, she thought, so why do I have to waste my time doing this?

Today, we now take it as a first priority in any instruction session to explicitly answer the question, Why on earth should any of you care about anything I'm about to say to you during this session? and keep that in mind with each outcome of the session. For some freshman classes, Kevin has even written,

"Why should I care about the library?" on the board at the beginning of the session and used that as a framing device for the class's specific learning outcomes. This approach is just one way to instantiate the learner-centered idea that, unless we can answer the who cares question in a way that makes sense to the learners, we've failed to be autonomy supportive in the relevant sense.

In truth, as educators, we *are* (at least on the face of it) making students do something they don't necessarily want to do (e.g., go to the library, write a research paper, etc.), which is not exactly what we think about as autonomy supportive, but it is necessary in order to have a curriculum, a class, or even an institution of higher education at large. So, as *learner-centered* educators, we have to constantly look for ways to engage in an empathic dialogue with learners to concretely demonstrate that we understand their perspective, respect them as people, and don't want to control them. One way to do this is to actually appeal to their autonomy and explain the reasons it might be worth it for them, from their own perspective and sense of value, to engage with the task we are asking of them. In effect, this strategy invites the learner to adopt the teacher's perspective on why the lesson is important, which the learner may be more inclined to internalize when it's framed in learner-centered language (e.g., "If you pay attention today, it can help you achieve your goals").

Aside from helping learners understand that research essentially is just looking up something that interests them, this concept can also be applied to critical-thinking skills, such as evaluating information. Discussing what makes a source reliable will look very different if our fundamental goal is to provide explanatory rationales to learners for why they could possibly care about an issue in the first place than if we just assume learners know why this is important and give them a handout on the CRAAP test.

One strategy we like to use when talking about evaluating information is to situate this issue within a broader context than just the assignment at hand or just the library. For example, we might say something like, "You're exposed to all kinds of stuff every day—information from CNN, Fox News, stuff your friend says to you at a party, stuff your uncle tells you at a wedding, things you read on blogs or in *Us Weekly* or on *TMZ*—how do you go about figuring out that, *This* is something I'm going to believe or *This* is something it seems I should be skeptical about?"

In our experience, learners often already know the answer to this kind of question. They might say something about experts or reliable sources being trustworthy for everyday kinds of belief construction. For example, if you need help answering a legal question, you consult a lawyer; if you break your leg, you go to a doctor; and if you need your transmission rebuilt, you go to an auto mechanic. We then ask them to extend the same principle to scholarly information: "Okay, so if you have a question about how to improve your self-esteem, who would you look to?" "A psychology researcher," students will usually say. "And where do you find that information?" we might then ask. Inevitably, some student says, "Well, the library, right?" which often opens up a conversation about the economics of information: "Look, you gotta use the library because we all have a desire to have credible beliefs, and we can usually only find this kind of information (for example, what a psychology professor has written about self-esteem) in a library because [insert your preferred explanation of the cost of information]."[19]

This approach may be very similar to what many librarians will typically say about these matters. The key difference is the fundamental goal of this technique—to relate to learners on their own terms. This means that we don't just explain why it's objectively important to understand the economics of information, but why the economics of scholarly information might be relevant to their lives and the things they care about. This twist on framing the problem in an autonomy-supportive style allows us to both nurture a learner's inner motivational resources *and* meet our information literacy learning outcomes. The pedagogical difference is a subtle one between autonomy and control, but it has enormous implications for a learner's psychology, motivation, and ultimately, learning.

3. USE NONCONTROLLING LANGUAGE AND BEHAVIOR

Browse just about any self-help book written in the last few years and you're likely to see an application of some empirical principles from contemporary cognitive behavioral therapy outlining the psychological dangers of *oughts* and *shoulds*. When our self-talk involves thoughts such as, You should've woken up much earlier today to work on this chapter! we may think this is natural way of speaking to ourselves. However, from a psychological standpoint, these kinds of statements can be emotionally paralyzing. This is almost certainly because this kind of negative self-talk takes the form of authoritative commands. Rather than coming from a place of choice, freedom, or self-love, *shoulds* invoke the language of external motivation and controlling behavior: You ought to do something, whether you want to or not! (And, it's often implied, You are *bad!*) It's as though we've internalized the voice of an adversarial figure, a drill sergeant we've allowed to permanently live inside our minds and hearts, and have taken it upon ourselves to carry out their demands.

Though we have anecdotally heard many people suggest that without this kind of negative self-talk and external pushing it's difficult for them to become motivated, the research suggests that this kind of motivational language actually stifles desire. Over the long haul, intrinsic motivation and an internal language based on interest, passion, and curiosity drives us to want to do things at a far higher rate than the language of *oughts*. As far back as 1961, Carl Rogers made a similar point about motivation, writing that as individuals in distress grow in the therapeutic relationship, they tend to move away from such language and behavior.[20] Interestingly, Rogers explicitly invokes the language of autonomy and intrinsic motivation, noting that telling people what they *should* do and how they *ought* to behave—as well as an individual's introjection of these controlling styles—not only thwarts intrinsic motivation, but leads to psychological maladjustment, low self-esteem, and a lower quality of life more generally.

Consequently, learner-centered educators seeking to create an autonomy-supportive environment for learners will want to purposely avoid this kind of language. "You should change your topic" is far less motivationally effective than something like "I think we could really expand on your initial idea to do something cool with it and make it even more specific" or "You know, sometimes a great way to approach this is to just think about what interests you about the topic. Do you have any phobias [or insert any other research topic assignment here]?" "You know, in situations like this, I find that PSYC-Info is often super useful because [. . .]" is far less controlling than "You should use PSYCInfo since our Discovery Layer is no good for this type of research." This doesn't mean we need to be overly politically correct and watch everything we say. But the research does suggest that the language we use matters when trying to facilitate a learner's experience rather than control it.

And it's not just words that matter. So does our behavior. In fact, we've found that what we've learned from the research on controlling behaviors has brought about significant changes in our own reference and instructional practices, leading to a revision in practices that we hadn't even realized were controlling. One example from Reeve struck us as especially compelling. It would be an example of a motivationally ineffective controlling behavior, Reeve writes, to take a pen or brush out of a learner's hand and show him the correct way to write or paint something when he was having difficulty, unless he asked you to do so.²¹ When we thought about the information literacy context, several parallels immediately came to mind, and frankly, were initially surprised by where they led us.

For example, we assume that very few of us would think it's particularly controlling to take a book off a shelf for a patron when we volunteer to help find a call number in the stacks. However, Kevin recently decided to stop doing this, for the precise reason that it's interfering with the learner's ability to act in a free, autonomous way. Instead, Kevin now makes a conscious effort to let the learner find the book and take it off the shelf herself. He will, of course, help the patron, explain how everything works, and even guide her to the proper shelf when necessary. But he no longer takes the book off the shelf or points to the book when he's located it first (which is usually the case). It's a more autonomy-supportive approach that allows the learner to take responsibility for her own learning.

Similarly, at every library we've worked in (almost ten between the two of us), reference librarians tend to do all the typing when helping a patron find a resource in the catalog or a library database. They always turn the computer toward the students so that they can see and follow along, but rarely, if ever, have we seen entire interactions where learners were encouraged to do all the typing for themselves, with the librarian simply as their guide. But at Kevin's most recent place of employment, he noticed that they did something very different: librarians walk patrons over to a computer specifically used for teaching purposes, sit down with them, and let them do all the typing and searching for themselves, with the librarian's guidance. When he saw this, Kevin thought of Reeve's example of taking the pen out of a student's hand, and he realized that even the most well-intentioned among us can slip into a controlling style. It makes such a big difference to sit *with* a learner, instead of sitting behind a reference desk while allowing the learner to see what we're typing on an angled computer screen. Even from an outside perspective, sitting with a learner looks more like a genuine partnership than when a librarian is typing and pointing at a screen for the patron. There are likely many examples of moments like this in each of our everyday work lives, and taking the time to reflect on them can make a significant difference in the type of learning environment we are creating for our learners.

4. DISPLAY THE PATIENCE REQUIRED TO ALLOW LEARNERS TO WORK AT THEIR OWN PACE

Suppose you love pizza, and we say to you, "Look, we're going to buy you a slice from your favorite pizza place. The only catch is that you have to eat it as fast as possible." Instead of thinking, Awesome, PIZZA! you'd probably think, Well, pizza *does* sound great, but why can't I take my time and eat it the way I want, at my own pace? I think I'll pass.

This example brings out the important point that, although you might be allowed to do something you deem authentic, if you aren't allowed to do it in a relatively autonomous way, your intrinsic motivation will likely be undermined. If you get to eat the pizza at your own pace, you are excited, but if you have to rush it and not be able to enjoy it, what's really the point in doing it?

The same is true of learning. If you were to tell us that you'd like to commission us to lead a half-day workshop on autonomy-supportive pedagogy for your instruction department, we'd be happy to do so. But if you told us you'd like it to happen tomorrow, we'd probably be none too thrilled. We would want to take the time to learn about your department, talk about your individual needs, and arrange our travel in advance to work with the schedules of our respective families. We'd feel controlled by the time constraint in this scenario and be motivated by a sense of panic rather than of excitement for working with you that we'd normally have. You'd expect the work to suffer!

In the same way, an important element of autonomy-supportive pedagogy is doing our best to help learners work at their own pace. This can happen in any number of ways. Often, when working with a learner who is slow on the computer, it's easy, unless we're mindful of our patience and empathy, to think, Come on already! We might want to do the search for the learner, or we might develop a sense of frustration that can get in the way of treating the learner with the compassion and empathy she deserves (it can be easy to want the learner to go away rather than to dig in our librarian heels for a long session leading to significant learning). It's the same impulse when we are helping a patron find a book. It's easy to grab the book off the shelf for him since we've done it so many times that we can find it right away. But it's precisely because we've done it so many times that we can spot a book right away, and we don't want to deprive the learner of the experience and reward of discovering it for himself. These examples are nothing groundbreaking, but they illustrate what seems to be a natural tendency for most of us toward control, and they reinforce that patience and empathy can be required to engage in autonomy-supportive behavior.

Recently, Kevin encountered a situation that he resolved by appealing directly to the research on self-paced learning. It was his first time teaching a for-credit information literacy class at his new job. All the students in his class spoke English as their second (or third or fourth . . .) language. Kevin was given a syllabus for the class, which included the information literacy learning outcomes outlined by the college but still had significant leeway for how to conduct the class and what specifically to teach. Since this was his first time teaching a class at this school, Kevin decided to take a looser approach than normal and allow some flexibility with the schedule so he could get a sense of where the students were and allow them to work at their own pace.

Kevin had a significant learning curve during the first few weeks, but things finally settled down, and he began to get into a rhythm and develop a rapport with his students. However, as the semester wound down, he realized that he was way behind for the final assignment. Each worksheet the class completed throughout the semester was scaffolded to build toward an annotated bibliography, but time had run out to pull all the pieces together for the culminating project. Despite knowing that he'd approached the class in a way that was good for students, and that they had accomplished all the learning goals minus the annotated bibliography, Kevin still felt enormous pressure that he "should" do what he'd said on the syllabus and hold the students responsible for the final project.

Kevin spoke to his supervisor and mentor at the college, who had experience teaching the same class and was also teaching a section that same semester. When Kevin explained what was going on, his supervisor suggested that she was actually in the same boat, and after discussing the importance of, and the research about, allowing learners to work at their own pace, decided it was fine to cut the culminating final project. The students had learned all the skills and concepts that had been set out at the beginning of the course, so why force things? It was a strong example of research leading us to do the right thing by our learners—as well as the value of having empathic, learner-centered colleagues to support us!

5. ACKNOWLEDGE LEARNERS' NEGATIVE AFFECT

Back in ninth grade, Kevin happened to mention, out loud and in the middle of a class discussion on *To Kill a Mockingbird*, that he thought the book was stupid. Kevin's teacher responded to his wonderfully thoughtful literary criticism by saying, "You know what, *you're* stupid!" before realizing that this could get her in big trouble and backpedaling to clarify that sometimes his *behavior* was stupid (and really, even now, who could reasonably disagree?).

Educational psychologists would call what Kevin said about *To Kill a Mockingbird* an "expression of negative affect": a learner voicing negative feelings about school or schoolwork. For reasons he doesn't even remember anymore, Kevin was not connecting with the book and shared his feelings with his teacher in an admittedly angsty and inarticulate way. But this is by no means a unique situation to encounter in teaching and learning.

A few years ago, Kevin was helping some AP English students to do research on Faulkner's *The Sound and the Fury*, and he opened the session by asking the students what they thought about the book. It was, really, just an offhanded question. *The Sound and the Fury* is one of Kevin's favorite novels, so he was genuinely curious what the students thought about it. Their comments were, quite overwhelmingly, negative: "Ugh, I hate it!" "Why's it so hard?!" "Dude, what's the deal with *Quentin?!*"

Kevin could tell that this embarrassed the teacher, but these thoughts really amused him. In fact, more than that, he was *interested* in them. In a very nonjudgmental tone, he asked one student *why* she hated the book. He wondered what the student made of the reasons Faulkner might have chosen to write the book in a way that made it kind of hard. What was that narrative style trying to accomplish? And he wanted to know what was so confusing about Quentin's behavior that we'd have to wonder what his deal is.

Rather than being counterproductive pedagogically (at first, it seemed like irrelevant banter to the students), this approach opened up productive discussions that served as authentic avenues of research for the students. For example, the student who was confused about Quentin's "deal" ended up doing research and finding articles on Quentin's conflict between the rules of the society he grew up in and his desire to be his own person. One student, who had told Kevin the reason she hated Faulkner was that her teacher was making her write a paper she didn't feel like writing (asserting her desire for complete autonomy), ended up writing about death. "Well, what do you like to think about?" Kevin asked her, to which she replied, "Death, Kevin. I spend a lot of time thinking about death." "Sweet," Kevin said. "Try typing in *death* to the library catalog, and let's see what we find."

The student found a book called *The Oxford Handbook of Philosophy of Death* and some articles on Faulkner's treatment of death in his novels and was good to go with some research that reflected her true self (i.e., a confused teenager obsessed with death). Though she initially approached him with a snarky attitude, she ended up writing Kevin a follow-up e-mail thanking him for the time he'd spent working with her on her research. Having her actual interest taken seriously—even if it was meant to be slightly shocking—not only broke down the student's emotional wall, but allowed her to connect with an assignment she'd initially had no interest in completing.

This success with helping students see that research really *could* be about them and their own lives, even within the context of something seemingly as foreign to them as Faulkner, was initiated in an off-the-cuff way by a willingness to accept and even openly embrace learners' expressions of negative affect about their schoolwork. It's not hard to see the reason this makes such a difference. We're *people*, after all. Who among us likes every single thing that we're exposed to? It's only natural to have likes and dislikes, many of which will inevitably bubble up in the learning context. So when, as library educators, we can recognize a learner's potentially negative feelings about research in addition to the positive ones, we can often address them in productive ways. Negative feelings toward school need not lead to negative outcomes; in fact, they can be a catalyst for significant learning.

Letting Students Take the Lead: Authentic Learning and Autonomy Support

A teaching style that incorporates support for students to explore their authentic selves and to exercise their autonomy provides a strong framework for students to learn in a meaningful and sustained way. Librarians are in unique position to encounter learners primarily in the moment of some information need, and we can take the step back to help learners to recognize themselves and their agency in the research process.

In approaching interactions with learners from an autonomy-supportive and authentic standpoint, consider keeping the following reflective questions in mind:

- How am I allowing learners to see their true selves reflected in the task at hand?
- Am I allowing learners enough room to find themselves in the task? Have I prescribed too strict a framework for students to work within? Too broad?
- How can I acknowledge challenges and struggles while helping learners to move forward?
- Have I explained the point of what we are doing in terms of learners' own interests?
- Have I eliminated *ought* and *should* from my vocabulary?

- Am I rushing learners through their process or allowing them to take all the time they need?

Each of these questions is aimed at increasing student autonomy and creating a pedagogical space for learning driven by individual inner resources. By letting students take the lead in the learning process, we set the stage for significant learning interactions.

It's important to note, though, that what we've said in this chapter doesn't mean we must relax our standards in any way—after all, information literacy involves thinking *well* about information that matters to the learner. While we support learners' authentic interests in an autonomy-supportive environment, being oneself doesn't entitle anyone to an A. The end result does matter—did the student think well about his research question? Did he use reliable evidence to support his claims and arguments? In chapter five, we further discuss process and encouraging students to stretch toward a successful outcome. In the next chapter though, we take the next step in thinking about how to plan out learning interactions aimed at long-term retention and transfer.

NOTES

1. E. L. Deci and R. Flaste, *Why We Do What We Do: Understanding Self-Motivation* (New York: Penguin Books, 1996), 2–4.

2. M. H. Kernis and B. M. Goldman, "A Multicomponent Conceptualization of Authenticity: Theory and Research," in *Advances in Experimental Social Psychology*, vol. 38, ed. Mark P. Zanna (San Diego, CA: Academic Press, 2006), 283–357; R. J. Schlegel, J. A. Hicks, J. Arndt, and L. A. King, "Thine Own Self: True Self-Concept Accessibility and Meaning in Life," *Journal of Personality and Social Psychology* 96, no. 2 (2009): 473–90.

3. R. May, *The Discovery of Being: Writings in Existential Psychology* (New York: Norton, 1983), 69.

4. C. R. Rogers, "To Be That Self One Truly Is: A Therapist's View of Personal Goals," in *On Becoming a Person: A Therapist's View of Psychotherapy*, ed. C. R. Rogers (New York: Houghton Mifflin, 1961), 186.

5. R. M. Ryan and E. L. Deci, "Autonomy Is No Illusion: Self-Determination Theory and the Empirical Study of Authenticity, Awareness, and Will," in *Handbook of Experimental Existential Psychology*, ed. G. Jeff, L. K. Sander, and T. Pyszczynski (New York: Guilford, 2004), 449–79.

6. P. S. Bresnan, *Awakening: An Introduction to the History of Eastern Thought* (Upper Saddle River, NJ: Prentice Hall, 1999), 73–74.

7. J. Nakamura and M. Csikszentmihalyi, "The Concept of Flow," in *Flow and the Foundations of Positive Psychology* (Netherlands: Springer 2014), 239–63.

8. Schlegel et al., "Thine Own Self."

9. Kernis and Goldman, "A Multicomponent Conceptualization," 46.

10. Schlegel et al., "Thine Own Self," 473.

11. N. E. Perry, J. C. Turner, and Debra K. Meyer, "Classrooms as Contexts for Motivating Learning," in *Handbook of Educational Psychology*, ed. P. A. Alexander and P. H. Winne (New York: Routledge, 2006), 333.

12. S. N. Elliott, T. R. Kratochwill, J. L. Cook, and J. F. Travers, *Educational Psychology: Effective Teaching, Effective Learning* (Boston: McGraw-Hill, 2000), 66–67.

13. A. Assor, H. Kaplan, and G. Roth, "Choice Is Good, but Relevance Is Excellent: Autonomy-Enhancing and Suppressing Teacher Behaviours Predicting Students' Engagement in Schoolwork," *British Journal of Educational Psychology* 72, no. 2 (2002): 261–78.

14. A. Aviram and A. Assor, "In Defence of Personal Autonomy as a Fundamental Educational Aim in Liberal Democracies: A Response to Hand," *Oxford Review of Education* 36, no. 1 (2010): 111–26.

15. K. M. Klipfel, "Authentic Engagement: Assessing the Effects of Authenticity on Student Engagement and Information Literacy in Academic Library Instruction. *Reference Services Review* 42, no. 2 (2014): 229–45.

16. J. Reeve, "Why Teachers Adopt a Controlling Motivating Style Toward Students and How They Can Become More Autonomy Supportive," *Educational Psychologist* 44, no. 3 (2009): 159–75.

17. Ibid, 162–63.

18. Ibid, 168–71.

19. D. Fallis, "On Verifying the Accuracy of Information: Philosophical Perspectives," *Library Trends* 52, no. 3 (2004): 463–87.

20. C. R. Rogers, "To Be That Self One Truly Is."

21. Reeve, "Why Teachers Adopt."

EMPATHY AND THE
SCIENCE OF LEARNING

Lessons from the Cognitive Literature

Empathy and Cognitive Science:
An Unexpected Partnership

There are many beliefs about generational differences in technology usage, one of the most prevalent is about digital natives, individuals who grew up in the Internet Age and who can intuitively navigate the information landscape. The fascinating thing about this narrative is that it's simply not true:

Prominent educational psychologists Paul A. Kirschner and Jeroen J. G. van Merriënboer refer to this belief about digital natives as a "pervasive urban legend" in education. The trouble with urban legends is that we often take their truths for granted, despite the fact that they may have no basis in empirical reality. Nevertheless, one of the most prevalent and persistent educational urban legends lies directly at the heart of today's librarianship: Recent studies have demonstrated that critical-thinking skills applied to information (what we call information literacy) are neither simple nor

> **IN THIS CHAPTER, WE**
>
> - introduce readers to the cognitive complexities that learners face acquiring information literacy skills.
>
> - investigate the central role of empathy in the learning process from a cognitive perspective.
>
> - review current findings from the cognitive science literature and apply them to information literacy instruction.

instinctive. Kirschner and van Merriënboer write, "Although students are often thought of as being competent or even expert in information problem solving . . . because they are seen searching the web daily, research reveals that solving information problems is for most students a major if not insurmountable cognitive endeavor." The researchers then call out searching, finding, and processing information as challenging cognitive tasks that require significant training.[1]

This, of course, is something just about every working librarian knows, but it's nice to have our experience as practitioners validated by leading research in the field of educational psychology. At the same time, however, this research serves as a significant professional challenge for us. Recall that in chapter one we located the practice of empathy—approaching teaching guided by the question, What is it like to be a person learning something?— at the heart of learner-centered pedagogy. And one answer to the central question of this book comes from what may initially seem like a surprising source: the field of cognitive science. Though the cognitive lens is often thought of as a cold and dispassionate way of viewing human behavior, we believe this need not be so. It just depends on how you look at it. In this chapter, we outline a way of understanding the cognitive science of learning as deeply humanistic and a key tool for applying our Rogerian view of teaching.

Here is the basic problem as we see it: Educational research suggests that information literacy learning is an enormously difficult cognitive process that many learners find intellectually overwhelming. Simply put, information literacy skills are so complex that learners' brains have a hard time processing them. The information literacy librarian's challenge, then, is not *just* to teach information literacy skills in a way that seems intuitive or in the way we were taught by other practitioners. Rather, as learner-centered educators, we must recognize that our learners' brains are challenged to learn information skills and must seek to make this task as easy as possible for them from a cognitive standpoint. We also need to keep in mind that students will be approaching these questions from a different state of understanding than the librarian. We are experts in information, they are beginners, so how do we bridge this gap? By shifting the focus away from ourselves as teachers and thinking about *the process of learning*, we gain important insight into facilitating learning in a learner-centered manner (recall our discussion about facilitating learning versus being the "sage on the stage" at the beginning of chapter one).

Although we do see the cognitive complexity of information literacy learning as a significant challenge for teaching librarians, the good news is the same literature that raises this instructional challenge for us—empirical research into the science and psychology of learning—also helps us articulate and put into practice evidence-based solutions. By seeking to understand who our learners are, in a deep psychological sense, we can help them become more successful. Used in this way, cognitive science can help us answer a fundamentally learner-centered question—What is it like to be a person learning something?—and ground our teaching in an evidence-based practice of empathy. As we see it, an approach to teaching information literacy based on the science of learning is empathic because it considers the learner's perspective *as a learner* to be primary. We put ourselves in our learners' shoes (or heads, as it were), try to understand which strategies help them learn and which do not, and base our practices on cognitive principles that promote learning.

Here we see a concrete implication of a key tenet of our learner-centered approach as stated in chapter one: *who we are as people matters*. Learners are not empty vessels to be filled with knowledge, but human beings with a unique set of cognitive capacities. When we begin to apply this principle to the information literacy context, we see the pedagogical necessity of understanding how learners' brains process information. One thing we find interesting about this realization is that it's another instance where we really begin to notice just how radical a commitment learner-centered teaching is. We may not have guessed when we signed up for library school (or even many years into our careers) that being a librarian involves developing a relatively sophisticated practical understanding of learning and the brain. But this is what learner-centered pedagogy seems to demand from us.

For the rest of this chapter, we discuss six principles about teaching drawn from the educational psychology literature. We start off each principle by explaining the theory and research behind it, then move on to concrete applications for the information literacy librarian. To facilitate the demonstration of what these ideas look like in practice, we apply them to a hypothetical course, modeling a common library instruction scenario, and provide templates you can use to apply these principles to your practice as a learner-centered instructor.

Six Cognitive Principles for Organizing Information Literacy Instruction

For the purposes of this chapter, let's imagine we've been contacted by a faculty member who wants to bring her lower-level writing class into the library for instruction. We receive the following e-mail:

> Dear librarian,
>
> This semester I am teaching English 101: Introduction to College Writing. The students will be writing a research paper for their final project. They can choose any topic of their interest to research but need to come up with a novel argument. I'd like to bring them to the library at the beginning of the semester to learn how to use the library, find good sources for their paper, and make citations.
>
> My class meets on Monday, Wednesday, and Friday from 9–9:50. Please let me know if you can accommodate this request!
>
> Thanks,
> Professor X

In this example, we don't receive additional information about the assignment from the instructor—it really is that open-ended. We work through an approach to this example over the course of the rest of this chapter following these six cognitive principles:

1. Limit learning outcomes.
2. Focus on a problem to solve.
3. Build a narrative.

4. Activate background knowledge.
5. Focus on deep structure.
6. Active learning is practice of deep structure.

PRINCIPLE 1. LIMIT LEARNING OUTCOMES

Often when preparing a session, a librarian might think, But I don't have enough time to teach all the skills the faculty member wants the students to learn! That is certainly true in our imaginary class, where the librarian has only fifty minutes to teach the students how to use the library, how to find sources for their final paper, and how to create consistent citations. So, what is the librarian to do? The temptation is to pack as much content as librari-an-ly possible into the fifty-minute session to maximize students' exposure to the resources offered by the library. And, since this may be our only chance to interact with these students, we'd better make sure to hit on a lot of the research skills they need, both conceptual and practical, too! It may come as a surprise, then, that the cognitive literature indicates this content-maximizing strategy has learning-minimizing returns, with students retaining much less as the amount of content increases. Instead, research tells us that instructors can maximize student learning by minimizing the amount of information presented in class. In other words, it's more important to go in depth on a topic than to cover a wide breadth of topics, thus allowing students to learn one thing well rather than many things not at all well (or just not at all).

Ever since the Internet exploded the world of information into an ever-expanding vastness, the phrase *information overload* has entered the popular vocabulary. This phenomenon occurs when people are presented with too much information to parse out and prioritize what will actually be useful to them. Psychologists and information scientists have studied this affliction of the information age and hypothesized that people will engage in coping behaviors to mitigate its overwhelming effects, such as tuning out information or being satisfied with good enough rather than the best information (called "satisficing" behavior).

While we often think about information overload as happening when we retrieve something like a million results in a Google search, it can also happen on a smaller (but similarly impactful) scale in the classroom. The human brain can only take in so much information at a time, as the knowledge must make connections to previously learned information for the brain to make sense of it. So when instructors try to pack as much content as possible into a class session, the students only take in a fraction of it before their brains turn off. It's not laziness—it's biology!

Here's the science behind this concept. There are three major types of memory: sensory memory, which is virtually instantaneous and which we experience through our five major senses; working memory, the part of the brain that engages with what you are currently thinking about; and long-term memory, which is where we store knowledge for later retrieval and use. For learning to occur, information must travel from working memory to long-term memory. But working memory is only so big (though exactly how big is a decades-long scientific debate), and if it gets filled up, then any additional information has no chance of making it to long-term memory (bringing truth to the saying "in one ear and out the other"). In sum, only the amount of information that can fit into a person's working memory has a chance of being learned.

This understanding of the brain's capacity and processing capability has direct implications for the classroom. If we know that any given individual can only learn a certain number of concepts at one time, then it is our responsibility as learner-centered educators to adjust our teaching accordingly. By targeting only two or three learning outcomes per instruction session, library instructors can minimize the cognitive load placed on the student, thus increasing the likelihood of learning. Though it may seem counterintuitive at first glance, minimizing content can maximize learning (whereas maximizing content *will* decrease learning).

Theory into Practice

In a library instruction scenario, it can be a struggle to select only two or three learning outcomes to focus on during a class. One way to intentionally process and plan your session is to write out *all* the potential learning outcomes that would be useful for students to gain during their library session and then whittle them down to the essentials, keeping the following questions in mind:

- Where are students in the research process when they come to the library for instruction?
- What are the core skills students will need to succeed in their research assignment?
- Will there be other opportunities to reach students outside of this session (or to advocate for additional instruction sessions)?

In most cases, this will be an iterative process—it's not easy to narrow down outcomes to essentials, especially when our very understandable impulse is to at least expose students to all the content they may potentially find useful.

Let's turn back to our classroom example to work through this process. We've agreed to lead a library instruction session for English 101, where students are writing a research paper on a topic of their choosing. What are all the possible learning outcomes we would want students to walk away with in this course? We think it might look something like this:

Students will be able to

- contact a librarian if they have additional questions about their research.
- feel comfortable and welcome in the library.
- define an appropriately sized research question about a topic they are interested in.
- explore various aspects of their topic.
- develop keywords that lead them to information on their topic.
- employ Boolean operators and other search strategies to construct a meaningful and precise search.
- use library databases to find information on their topic.
- use the Open Web to find information on their topic.
- determine the relevance and utility of sources for an argument.
- evaluate the reliability and nature of a source.
- utilize a constellation of appropriate sources to develop an argument, as well as to refute potential counterarguments.
- ethically use sources and employ a consistent citation style.

That's a dozen learning outcomes right off the bat, and you can probably imagine even more you'd consider crucial for student success on this assignment. Even if we had infinite time in the library session, we couldn't address all these outcomes because, as we've outlined above, students wouldn't be able to absorb so much information all at once. With that in mind, we apply the framing questions to our list of outcomes to begin the narrowing down process.

The first question is, *Where are students in the research process when they come to the library for instruction?* Based on what we know about the class, the students are coming in at the beginning of the semester, so they may not know exactly what they will be writing about. It seems likely they will all be at the beginning of their research process (a fact, of course, we can and should confirm with the English 101 instructor). We begin by eliminating the outcomes that would be too far along in the process to be particularly helpful to someone just beginning to investigate their topic:

- contact a librarian if they have additional questions about their research
- feel comfortable and welcome in the library
- define an appropriately sized research question about a topic they are interested in
- explore various aspects of their topic
- develop keywords that lead them to information on their topic
- employ Boolean operators and other search strategies to construct a meaningful and precise search
- ~~use library databases to find information on their topic~~
- ~~use the Open Web to find information on their topic~~
- ~~determine the relevance and utility of sources for an argument~~
- ~~evaluate the reliability and nature of a source~~
- ~~utilize a constellation of appropriate sources to develop an argument, as well as to refute potential counterarguments~~
- ~~ethically use sources and employ a consistent citation style~~

Bam! We've already eliminated half our outcomes, getting us closer to a workable basis for a lesson plan. This is usually the moment that panic sets in: But students are going to need to know and do all these things to succeed in this assignment! We understand this concern, and the way we've dealt with it in our own instructional practice is by realizing that the learning outcomes you are cutting out right now can still come in handy later.

For example, we both have used them, at different colleges and universities at different times, to advocate and design follow-up information literacy sessions during the same semester. When an instructor sees that we have a good understanding of student learning, what will be productive in a class period, and how our instruction has helped learners succeed, we've found that multiple sessions and ongoing, collaborative partnerships have been the frequent result. At the very least, no faculty member has ever refused to share ancillary materials with their students. Leftover outcomes may serve as the basis for creating asynchronous materials for students in the class. These can often be shared with the instructors so they can find other ways of incorporating the skills over the course of the semester. Thus, we've found that we still get to address most (if not all) of the learning outcomes we think are important to meet in some way, shape, or form.

Now, back to our list. We still have six outcomes left, at least two (or possibly three) more than we'd ideally like to work with in a single session. So let's apply our next question:

What are the core skills students will need to succeed in their research assignment?

- contact a librarian if they have additional questions about their research
- feel comfortable and welcome in the library
- define an appropriately sized research question about a topic they are interested in
- ~~explore various aspects of their topic~~
- develop keywords that lead them to information on their topic
- employ Boolean operators and other search strategies to construct a meaningful and precise search

Applying this question led to the removal of only one outcome; while it is important for students to examine various facets of their topic in developing their research question, for a first-year course they likely don't need to conduct as deep a dive into their topic as students farther along in their studies. This outcome might also be partially addressed in creating the research question.

Now we are down to just five outcomes and have one more narrowing question to ask: *Will there be other opportunities to reach students outside of this session?* The answer here, in many cases, is yes: whether through creating a handout, putting together a quick online course guide, or simply putting your contact information on the course syllabus, there are usually ways to extend your reach beyond the single library session. With those options in mind, we can narrow down to three remaining outcomes:

- ~~contact a librarian if they have additional questions about their research~~
- feel comfortable and welcome in the library
- define an appropriately sized research question about a topic they are interested in
- develop keywords that lead them to information on their topic
- ~~employ Boolean operators and other search strategies to construct a meaningful and precise search~~

We can add librarian contact information to a syllabus or course guide (or better yet, both), so we don't need to have that explicit outcome in the session. Creating a welcoming space in the library, however, is an affective outcome that relies on the persona of the librarian in the class to create. That's definitely one to keep for the in-person session (we discuss this in more detail in chapter four). On the other hand, creating the research question at the beginning of their process is going to be critical for students to do (and do well) and would benefit from examples given by the librarian, so we want to keep that one in. Boolean operators and procedural types of search strategies can be demonstrated effectively through an online guide or physical handout and can serve as a quick reference for students in the future. Finally, developing relevant and precise keywords is a critical component for student success in searching, an important element at the beginning of the research process, and a skill that could benefit from real-time feedback from the librarian and peers.

With our three questions answered, we've managed to go from a dozen outcomes to three:

- feel comfortable and welcome in the library
- define an appropriately sized research question about a topic they are interested in
- develop keywords that lead them to information on their topic

That's a reasonable number to accomplish during a class session, leaves cognitive space for students to actually learn them, and gives us time to have students practice these skills during a single class session. We're off to a good, learner-centered start!

You can see a consolidated view of this process in the graphic organizer (figure 3.1). A blank graphic organizer for your own course planning is available at www.alaeditions.org/webextras.

PRINCIPLE 2. FOCUS ON A PROBLEM TO SOLVE

For the librarian, every instruction session and reference interaction can be perceived as a puzzle. In planning library instruction, we use learning outcomes to put together a coherent picture of the research process. In a reference interview, we piece together information from the patron to form a question then gather information from a variety of sources to come to an answer. Many librarians point to these moments as their favorite part of the job, and perhaps it's no surprise. Problem solving is innately fun and engaging for us. For example, people enjoy solving jigsaw and crossword puzzles in their spare time; even our primate relatives like solving puzzles for their own sake. In a landmark 1949 study, scientists at the University of Wisconsin found that monkeys didn't require a prize in order to solve a simple puzzle; they found the process of solving the puzzle to be pleasure enough.[2]

One might call this the "Mary Poppins Principle": in every job that must be done, there is an element of fun. The challenge for us as librarians is to

FIGURE 3.1

WORKED "DO LESS" GRAPHIC ORGANIZER

What are all the possible outcomes you might want to cover in this session?	Where are students in the research process when they come to the library for instruction? **The Beginning of the Process**	What are the core skills that students will need to succeed in their research assignment?	Will there be other opportunities to reach students outside of this session? **Yes**
• Contact a librarian if they have additional questions about their research	• Contact a librarian if they have additional questions about their research	• Contact a librarian if they have additional questions about their research	• Feel comfortable and welcome in the library
• Feel comfortable and welcome in the library	• Feel comfortable and welcome in the library	• Feel comfortable and welcome in the library	• Define an appropriately sized research question about a topic they are interested in
• Define an appropriately sized research question about a topic they are interested in	• Define an appropriately sized research question about a topic they are interested in	• Define an appropriately sized research question about a topic they are interested in	• Develop keywords that lead them to information on their topic
• Explore various aspects of their topic	• Explore various aspects of their topic	• Develop keywords that lead them to information on their topic	
• Develop keywords that lead them to information on their topic	• Develop keywords that lead them to information on their topic	• Employ Boolean operators and other search strategies to construct a meaningful and precise search	
• Employ Boolean operators and other search strategies to construct a meaningful and precise search	• Employ Boolean operators and other search strategies to construct a meaningful and precise search		
• Use library databases to find information on their topic			
• Use the Open Web to find information on their topic			
• Determine the relevance and utility of sources for an argument			
• Evaluate the reliability and nature of a source			
• Utilize a constellation of appropriate sources to develop an argument, as well as to refute potential counterarguments			
• Ethically use sources and employ a consistent citation style			

turn what we're asking students to do into a puzzle of sorts, with stakes, boundaries, and the promise of some kind of satisfying resolution. If we structure the way we teach around solving a concrete intellectual problem, there is increased opportunity to engage with students.

This is the same reason that librarians tend to get a sinking feeling when asked to do a library session without a related class assignment. Implicitly, we understand that students are likely going to pay less attention if they don't have a specific reason, or one at all, to spend intellectual energy on the contrived task at hand. Having an assignment that is tied to the library session, on the other hand, immediately creates a problem context for the students: They want to succeed at their assignment, and the library session, if framed correctly by the librarian, can give them the tools for doing so. The stakes are set, so the motivation to pay attention may follow.

Finally, though it may seem obvious: one major lesson drawn from the cognitive literature is that people tend to remember what they pay attention to.[3] And, if we also know that people are more likely to be interested in things when they are presented as problems to be solved rather than a straight delivery of content (How do I get this book that I need if it's only at a library on the East Coast? rather than "And here is how you use ILL . . ."), then it follows that planning your session around specific problems related to a class assignment can improve learning and retention of concepts.

Theory into Practice

The simplest, most concrete way to establish a problem to solve in an instruction session is to ensure that every session you take on has an associated assignment. No more library sessions to "introduce students to the library," to cover while a professor goes to a conference, to show off a favorite database. Without an assignment, there is no problem to solve; without a problem to solve, why would students pay attention? We hereby grant you permission to politely decline to take these classes and to suggest that the requesting individuals bring their students to the library when they have an assignment that requires some element of research (you can even offer to help them create one!). We promise that, rather than upsetting the professor and souring your relationship, a brief explanation of why you want to do a more substantial session (using the information you've learned about cognitive engagement in this chapter) will, if our experiences are any indicator, go a long way toward establishing you as a legitimate, collaborative partner in the educational process.

Fortunately, in our example, Professor X has provided an assignment (however vague) that her students will be working on at the time they come into the library. The next step we can take is to make that problem context explicit to students by sharing the learning outcomes at the beginning of class and discussing *exactly* how those outcomes provide the means necessary for solving the assignment. We might write the outcomes on a white board before students come to class then use that as the launching-off point for the class:

> The focus of this session will be to help you learn the research skills you will need to complete this assignment. I was reading over your assignment, and I realized that the first thing you need to do is develop a college-level research question. I think this is actually one of the most challenging aspects of doing research—just getting started with figuring out what you're going to write about—so our focus today is just going to be on that, how to go about creating a good research question. This will get you set up nicely for the paper you're working on and help you out later in the semester. And I think this will help you in your other classes as well since most of the research assignments you'll do in college involve developing a good research question. So, what we do today will be really useful to you for the rest of your college career.

Having an assignment also allows the library instructor to tie high-level, abstract information literacy concepts to a concrete, real-world problem. For example, let's take the "Research as Inquiry" frame from the ACRL *Framework for Information Literacy for Higher Education*. As a profession, we have agreed that this concept is critical for students to grasp in order to have an understanding of how information is created, works, and is used. Our example assignment asks students to choose any topic of their interest to research. And how will they go about doing this in class? Through two out of our three learning outcomes: define an appropriately sized research question about a topic they are interested in *and* develop keywords that lead them to information on their topic. This takes the abstraction of research as a process of inquiry and breaks it into concrete steps that lead students to discover that idea for themselves. Additionally, with this high-level idea explicitly tied to a real-world problem, students can then see how and why they might use these skills in other circumstances (e.g., the next time they get a research assignment), which helps to facilitate transfer. As the research indicates, when students understand the relevance of a skill, they are better prepared to recognize structural similarities in other contexts, which may look different on the surface, but in which the same knowledge applies.

In sum, when planning a class, consider the following questions:

- Is there a course assignment that is related to the library session?
- Can you explicitly tie your learning outcomes to how they will help students solve the problem of their assignment?
- Is there language in the assignment you can use to amplify the importance of your learning outcomes?

As we've seen, when we answer these questions we can better help learners see the relevance of our instruction. By focusing on a problem to solve, we tap into an innately human cognitive capacity—our interest in puzzles and native impulse to resolve them.

PRINCIPLE 3. BUILD A NARRATIVE

Stories have a powerful hold over us as human beings. Author Joan Didion famously began her essay "The White Album" by asserting, "We tell ourselves stories in order to live." The narratives we tell ourselves about our world are both a coping mechanism and determinant for how we deal with the existential realities of our lives. We *are* our stories. This concept of story as central to the human experience, long familiar within the liberal arts, is becoming prevalent in psychology as well. In her influential TEDx talk on the importance of vulnerability, psychological researcher Brene Brown locates storytelling as a core part of human psychological flourishing. Citing her qualitative research on the phenomenology of shame, Brown argues that true human connection involves the willingness to be vulnerable, which requires us to share our stories—narratives involving who we really are—with trusted others. In this way, we develop the ability to "own our stories," or take accountability for things that have happened to us and who we now are, so that in the future we can choose who we want to be.[4] Brown's view fits squarely within the humanist tradition and echoes the Rogerian revolution in psychology outlined in chapter one.

The importance of story is just one more place we find humanism and cognitive science in agreement. In fact, just as we saw with puzzles, human beings are innately interested in stories, cognitively speaking. Specifically, empirical research shows that the human memory accords a special place to information presented in the form of a story. Educational psychologist Daniel Willingham writes that "psychologists refer to stories as 'psychologically privileged,' meaning that they are treated differently in memory than other types of [non-narrative] material."[5] When someone tells us a story, we remember the details better than when they're framed in a way that lacks cohesive narrative context. Information delivered in the narrative story format is a uniquely human preference, both humanistically and scientifically central to our emotional lives and the memories we make and retain.

Theory into Practice

This insight gives teacher-librarians a concrete, empirically based strategy for improving learning. When it is appropriate and necessary to offer explanations of class content to students, librarians may choose to embed their instruction within the context of a narrative since this maximizes the potential for learners to retain information. One effective storytelling strategy is what we call narrative modeling, where the library instructor walks learners through some component of the research process by modeling how they would effectively approach it. The librarian provides students with a compelling, step-by-step example they can then follow in their own research processes. If the librarian has followed the first two principles in this chapter, the example should already be relevant to the particular problem context the students face (their assignment) and focus on a manageable amount of content for the students to remember (e.g., developing a research question and keywords). Building on our first two principles, narrative modeling gives us one more strategy for getting students to retain information and concepts. Embedding information within the context of a story makes the presentation inherently interesting and memorable.

Narrative modeling lends itself quite naturally to information literacy instruction since demonstrations on how to use a particular resource or perform a specific skill have historically been, and remain, cornerstones of library instruction. Narrative modeling is a twist on this approach. Instead of a lecture on strategies at a broad level, the complex narrative details precisely how and why the librarian performed a given research task.

As with most strategies discussed in this book, narrative modeling is possible in a variety of information literacy pedagogical contexts, ranging from one-shot instruction to semester-long courses, from creating handouts to building digital learning objects. To illustrate the concrete differences between lecture and narrative modeling, we go back to our original example, the case of English 101 and Professor X, which will also demonstrate basic strategies that can be transferred to any instructional context you like.

So far in this chapter, we've limited our learning outcomes and set up a problem context for the session. We've kept learning as our focus and have organized things to set our learners up for success. Our next step is to deliver the instruction based on our learning outcomes. We begin by modeling a narrative.

When we receive an instruction request like the one from Professor X, at some point we start to figure out what our demo is going to be: how will we show our learners how to perform a given information literacy task? In this case, we need to model how to define an appropriately sized research question about a topic of interest.

Once, when faced with nearly the same instruction scenario as our example, Kevin woke up, ignored preparing for the class that he was teaching later that morning, and poured himself some cereal. As Kevin ate his Frosted Mini Wheats, he Googled the name of the Canadian rapper Drake. Drake's latest album had just been released, and Kevin started reading reviews of it.

At the time, this behavior just seemed to him like procrastination. Instead of doing the "real" work of preparing for class, Kevin started messing around on the Internet and looked up something he was interested in (he was super into Drake at the time). But then something hit him. Wasn't he trying to show his students that research is just looking up something that piques your curiosity and that you want to know more about? If this is the case, there really shouldn't be any difference between the kinds of things Kevin looked up over breakfast and the kinds of things he looked up later in a library database. Why was one "just" procrastination and the other "real" research? That seemed totally wrong, the complete opposite of what research really seemed all about and the complete opposite of what really mattered to him as a teacher.

As we defined it in chapter one, information literacy involves *thinking well about what matter*s. When he made a separation between what was suitable to look up at home versus what was suitable to look up at work, Kevin was not being very learner-centered. He had defined what matters as "what matters to super-important researchers doing super-important academic research stuff that sounds all scholarly" rather than "what matters *to a particular person*." In fact, he'd fallen into a trap that so many learners fall into themselves—the belief that their research must sound scholarly rather than simply follow a question that genuinely interests them.

This revelation turned things around and made Kevin realize that what he'd been doing that morning *was* the prep he was supposed to be doing. He grabbed an idea from one of the articles, expanded on it by doing a little additional research in the library catalog and article databases, and had the plan he needed for his class: a lesson that would model for students a true sense of research.

When it was time to begin his instruction during the class, Kevin started from the same place the students would be starting, situating himself within the exact problem context the students were currently facing. And thus Kevin commenced his narrative, which went something like this:

> So I think one of the most difficult things to do is just to get
> started, to figure out exactly what you're going to write about. I

was thinking about your assignment this morning, and I wasn't quite sure what I'd do for my research, so I just decided to forget about it and started looking up my favorite rapper, Drake. And I'm sitting there, just eating my breakfast, and then something interesting happened. I was reading this article—it's just a review of his new album—and it seems like a really silly article from kind of a scandalous entertainment news website called Vulture comparing Drake to Taylor Swift. [Kevin shows the article on the screen.[6]] But there was this passage that caught my attention, that made me think, Oh, wait, I think I could actually use this as the basis for my research.

The article talks about how Drake has kind of changed what it means to be authentic, or real, in hip-hop. Back in the day, with N.W.A. or Tupac and Biggie or whoever, to have a lot of cred in hip-hop, it was necessary to prove that you were authentically from the streets: you grew up in the inner city or you dealt drugs or you were in a gang or something like that. If you did those things, you were considered authentic or credible—a real, legitimate, hip-hop artist—and if you didn't, it could really hurt your legitimacy as a rapper. The same is true more recently for Jay Z, who grew up in the projects in Brooklyn and was a drug dealer growing up. But the article is saying that Drake has changed all that. Here's the sentence that caught my attention: [Kevin highlights the sentence on the screen.] "Drake's triumph, after all, has been to shift the terms of rap authenticity from Jay Z-style street bona fides to soul-baring honesty—to emotional authenticity, or at least the pretense of it."

When I read that sentence, I knew that this would make an interesting research topic: how Drake has been a catalyst for a major shift in hip-hop culture, moving it away from authenticity being about street cred to about just being honest about your feelings and who you really are. Hip-hop is now more about being yourself, no matter where you might happen to be from. And that's a really interesting shift in a major form of American popular music, one that I think is definitely worth exploring as research.

When Kevin created this narrative, he felt much better about his job as an instructor. He was showing students how to use the research process to look up things they actually might want to know about as people (which connects us once again to our learner-centered theme that *who we are as people matters*). With this approach, there is no difference between the private self and the school self. We are all just learners, ready to use the research process to think about things that matters to us.

Of course, creating a narrative requires technical skill. For example, think about the fact that Kevin knew the sentence he highlighted could potentially make a good research question. Put yourself in the students' shoes. Most students, especially ones in a class like English 101, won't automatically see how they could take the highlighted sentence and turn it into a full-blown research project. This is precisely where the librarian's experience and expertise come into play. As librarians, we've formed and have helped form countless research topics, taking basic ideas and generating complex questions and queries from them. Our task, as instructors, is to use our informational and pedagogical expertise to model for students how to develop a manageable research question that interests them seemingly out of nothing. This advanced skill is not something most people have, but librarians do.

This takes us back to the quote from Kirschner and van Merriënboer, which we began this chapter with, about the enormous cognitive complexity involved in becoming information literate. Instructors could just tell their students, "Make sure you choose a topic that interests you since you'll be working on it for a long time. Now let's move on to talk about . . . ." But for the most part, this strategy is ineffective. This assumes that students know how to develop a sophisticated research question based on things that matter to them, so the instructor may quickly move on to other matters. The problem is that most students *don't* know how to do this and won't until they practice it again and again. Constructing a quality research question is a major information literacy skill. In the absence of this skill, students will gravitate toward satisficing behavior: they'll do research on something that seems easy—"because there's information on it"—rather than on a true curiosity or passion. This is why modeling the successful behaviors that curious individuals employ to investigate their passions is so important. Without direct instruction and guided practice, students cannot be expected to develop such complex skills.

This challenge provides an excellent segue from the narrative introduced above to demonstrating the relevance of the next learning outcome—developing keywords—to the students in the class.

> So we see this really interesting shift in hip-hop culture, where Drake is redefining what being authentic in hip-hop means. Although this could be a totally legitimate focus of research, we also have certain expectations placed on us by the assignment prompt. For one thing, we're going to have to find reliable sources on our topic, ones that will help us explore it in an educated way, and back up what we're saying with good evidence. At this point, we more or less have a basic question to start with, and now it's about how we put the research together. And this is where some of the specific research skills we need to learn start to come in—they're ways to help us break things down so we can find information we need on a question that interests us. That's why this stuff is interesting, I think. Not because there's something super special about research skills, but because of what these research skills let you do: pursue questions that you actually care about. So, what we'll talk about now is how you go about doing that. How do I start breaking my topic down so I know the basic information that I'll need for my research? That's my next step: what are the main research concepts I'll be dealing with so that I can figure out what information I need to know and where I need to look for it?
>
> Well, I know that one of my major concepts, or what we often call keywords, is "Drake." So, right away, I know that Drake is going to be one of my major research concepts that I'll

need to investigate. So here, if I'm thinking about my research question, what I'm trying to figure out is what I need to know about Drake for the purposes of my topic. Well, I need some basic autobiographical information. Like, if Drake breaks the mold of a hip-hop artist, I know that in my paper I'm going to need to explain where he comes from, what his background is, and so forth. Just having done some basic research about Drake, I know that he's Canadian, he's part Jewish, and he was a child star on a Canadian teen melodrama—all really different elements of a hip-hop start from those of the so-called gangster rappers the article was talking about. So that will probably be a big component of my paper, and I'll need sources and information to back it up.

That seems to be the basic information I'll need about Drake's background and where I can find it. The next thing I started thinking about, when I was thinking about how I'd break my research question down, is that a main thing I need to know about is hip-hop and hip-hop culture. So something like "hip-hop" or "rap music" is going to be one of my keywords. And I know that since I'm talking about how hip-hop has changed and evolved from the way it used to be, maybe something about hip-hop history, one that kind of documents that progression, would be a really good source for me.

What I was actually thinking here is that a book would be a great resource for this since books are pretty broad and can cover a lot of ground. I thought maybe I'd see if I could find something about hip-hop history in the library catalog. And I actually found a great book about the history of hip-hop culture that is published by Yale University Press. Now I'm starting to get a bunch of really good sources together—ones about Drake and a book about hip-hop history published by a reputable academic press. This is what I meant earlier when I referred to how we put our question together and how we go about gathering our information. As long as we break down our question so we end up getting the information we need to examine it in an educated way, most any of the basic topics we think of will end up as things we can use in our research.

Ok, so my last major idea is about authenticity. That's really the central thread running through all my research—what does authenticity, or being yourself, really mean? For many hip-hop artists, it meant having street credibility. But for Drake, it seems to mean something like "just being yourself." He even has a line in one of his songs that says, "I'm authentic, real name, no gimmicks." So, I thought it would be interesting to explore the concept of authenticity and being yourself from several perspectives. I did some basic searching for the keyword "authenticity"—online and in the library databases—and it led me to lots of research, much of it from psychology, talking about how important authenticity and being yourself is to being happy. So I think that could be a really interesting focus on my paper— to ultimately use some research articles in psychology to show that this research actually supports Drake's concept of authenticity as a way to be happy. And if I did that, I'd have all different kinds of great resources—popular ones, an academic book or two, and some scientific research articles.

This is just a basic skeleton of what we might say during our imagined class, but the essential points of building a narrative around two of our major learning outcomes, developing a research question on a topic of interest and developing keywords, are all here. In this narrative, we modeled for students how to take a basic curiosity from life and turn it into a research question and to use keywords as building blocks to search for reliable information. This is information literacy as *thinking well about what matters* in action.

Since we hope that this narrative will only take up a short amount of our hypothetical session, much of the workshop will be devoted to students actively practicing these skills on their own research with the librarian's assistance (more on this later in the chapter). However, a final short narrative, summarizing the main takeaways of the class, is an effective way to hit our final learning outcome—that students feel welcome in the library and with librarians. This narrative might sound like this:

> You see, the things you're interested in are totally valid; it's just a matter of brainstorming your ideas and your research in a certain way. This is one of the main things that librarians can help you do. You can meet with us, and we can help you figure out what you might be interested in working on, how to turn that into a college-level research question, and then help you find good information and resources on it so that you'll have the sources and evidence you need for your paper. Please feel free to get in touch with me. You're more than welcome to just drop me a line or set up office hour appointments with me, just like you can do with your professors. It's not a weird thing to do—I meet with students all the time, so it's not like you'll be the only one doing it. I'm happy to sit down with you and help you figure out how to do your research. Research takes tons of practice, and one of the main advantages of working with a librarian is that we've got lots of practice doing this. We can be really useful in helping you through the same process that we talked about today: how to break down your topic and find information on it.

One major thing we're trying to do in this narrative example is expand learners' concepts of what counts as research. The example is manifestly not about being hip ("Oh, this guy is cool, he likes hip-hop!") or about trying to relate to students by guessing what their interests might be (as in, "Oh, Drake is really popular right now. I bet all the students will relate to this example, so they'll really pay attention"). In fact, there have been times when Kevin used this example and some students told him they don't like Drake. For instance, he once had a student who told Kevin that he strongly preferred Kendrick Lamar over Drake and thought Drake was kind of lame. The student, like Lamar, was from Compton, California, and identified much more with him than the Toronto-born Drake. This illustrates why it is important to stress that the narrative modeling is simply an example of the *strategies students can use to look up their own interests*, which can be transferred to the students' unique context. The important point, in case of the student in question, was that he saw how he could take his own interests—Kendrick Lamar and the role of Compton in his lyrics—and write about that. The goal, as discussed in chapter two, is to support learners' autonomy, rather than try to pick a cool topic for the student. This point is also important to stress throughout the class: "What we're focusing on is strategies that will work for you not only in this course, but any time you do research." This also furthers our goal of creating an interesting problem context that the students can identify with and facilitates helping students see how to transfer these skills outside of a particular classroom context.

This first narrative example is based on our hypothetical involving Professor X's assignment, an extremely open research project geared toward early-career students. Since many librarians, particularly subject liaison librarians, may face less freely structured instructional scenarios, it's worth briefly considering a more rigidly structured example as well.

Once Kevin was called upon to lead an instruction workshop for a senior-level class on geography research methods, a subject he was totally unfamiliar with. Kevin was clueless about what advanced research in the subject of geography looked like, being a liberal arts man from way back. So when he began preparing for the workshop, Kevin had no idea what kind of narrative he would model for the students, especially when he saw the topic the students were researching: the built environment. He didn't even know what it meant, much less how to model for students the strategies he would use to investigate his own interests in the matter.

Things started to turn around when Kevin looked up the phrase "built environment" in a general reference encyclopedia. It's a broad term referring to man-made living environments inhabited by humans. Okay, Kevin thought. That's a start, I guess. I mean, *I'm* a human. I *inhabit* a built environment. Maybe I have something to say about that.

Kevin started to think about his relationship to his built environment at the time, a small town in Northern California. And the first thing that came to mind was how he was a little bit unhappy living there. While most residents really loved the small-town feel, Kevin was used to larger-city environments. When he'd visited for his interview, Kevin envisioned himself having a little loft downtown, being able to walk to work in the morning and to restaurants at night, and taking part in the (small) city vibe. But for various reasons, that ended up not being possible (e.g., there were few downtown apartments), and it had a major impact on Kevin's happiness and quality of life. He wondered if there was any research on the walkability of a built environment and its impact on people's happiness. And sure enough, Kevin pretty quickly found an article on almost exactly this topic, which led him to lots of other great resources. He was then able to model a narrative, telling a politely modified version of his story, using the keywords "built environment," "walkability," and "happiness" or "quality of life." The session went well, and Kevin ended up meeting with several students from the class later to further help them work on their topics. This example nicely illustrates that, with a little creativity, it is possible to show learners how to connect one's interests to a topic, no matter the subject.

We've spent a lot of time in this chapter outlining the idea of narrative modeling because we think it's one of the most important and practical elements that teacher-librarians can incorporate into their practice. There are, however, times when narrative modeling alone may *not* be the best demo or lecturing strategy so we'll need to combine it with other methods.

For example, Kevin was recently teaching students in an eight-week information literacy course about the Dewey Decimal Classification system for the first time, and it seemed to him like narrative modeling was not an effective method for this kind of instruction. It could be a great method for explaining how to look up a book in the catalog, but it wasn't the best method for explaining what the Dewey Decimal system *is*. A conceptual explanation of what classification systems are and why they are necessary features of libraries didn't lend itself naturally to narrative modeling.

In this case, Kevin relied on a more traditional kind of storytelling delivery to help his students make sense of why a person might be interested in the inner workings of the Dewey Decimal system (which, let's face it, is probably not an intrinsically fascinating topic for students). This method, which we call *storytelling* (to distinguish it from *narrative modeling*), is also directly supported by the educational psychology literature. Researchers Arya and Maul, in a recent study, provide a concrete illustration of the difference between a traditional lecture and a storytelling narrative in the context of science education. A straightforward expository lecture on Galileo's discoveries might look like this:

> And with this simple, powerful tool [Galilean telescope], we can see many details when we use it to look up into the night sky. The moon may look like a smooth ball of light covered with dark spots, but on a closer look through this telescope, we can see deep valleys and great mountain ranges. Through the telescope, we can now see all the different marks on the moon's surface.[7]

This explanation, however, looks slightly different as a more traditional story:

> When Galileo looked through his new telescope, he could see the surface of the moon, and so he began his first close look into space. He slept during the day to work and see the moon at night. Many people thought that the moon was a smooth ball with a light of its own. Now that Galileo had a closer look through his telescope, he realized that the moon's surface had mountains and valleys.

The difference between the two modes of delivery is subtle, yet Arya and Maul's study indicates that the shift from lecture to story makes a significant difference for information retention and, thus, for student learning. It may not be entirely obvious how this could be applied to the library context, so let's go back to the Dewey example. One way Kevin could have introduced students to the material is this:

> The Dewey Decimal system was created by a librarian named Melvil Dewey as a way to organize information in libraries. It breaks down books in the library into ten different classes cor-

responding to a particular subject, which are then further broken down into subcategories. For example, if your book's call number starts with a Dewey Decimal number in the 150 range, you know that it's a psychology book. This is useful because it organizes all the books on the shelves together by topic, so when you go to find your book under 150, you can browse the shelf to find other books on similar topics right nearby. For example, if your book is on the psychology of self-esteem, there will probably be other books on the psychology of self-esteem to the right and left of yours.

While factually accurate, this description of Dewey's innovation for organizing books in libraries by topic is perhaps not the most compelling. Realizing that this might be a good time to experiment with illustrating a conceptual point about libraries through story, Kevin's explanation instead went something like this:

> So we're looking up books today, and I know some of you have noticed that there are these numbers you need to use to find your books in the library. We're definitely going to talk about how you go about actually finding a book, but first I want to talk a little bit about why we use these numbers.
>
> This thing happened to me once that I think is a good illustration of why we use numbers like this. One day when I was in library school, I came home from working at the library and my girlfriend had reorganized all my books . . . by color. All the orange books were together, and all the blue ones were together, and so forth. And I was like, "Dude, what did you do?! You organized my books by COLOR!" Can anyone guess why I wasn't too thrilled with this arrangement?
>
> Student response: "Yeah, well, how are you supposed to find anything?"
>
> Right! I was like, this is the worst way to organize books ever! I mean, it looks cute, I *guess*, but it's not very *useful*. How am I supposed to find the books I need?

So, something like this is actually why we use these numbers in the library. They're called Dewey Decimal numbers, and we use something called the Dewey Decimal System to organize the books in the library. It's named after this guy Melvil Dewey, who was a librarian working at a college library in Massachusetts in the late 1800s. Until this time, the most common way libraries shelved their books was by size and when the library got the book. So it was basically like, "Do you have any books on the American Revolution?" And the librarian had to be like, "Hmm, I think so. . . . Yeah, we've got a book on that. . . . It's the big green one we got in last Wednesday, I think."

The problem's exactly the same as my girlfriend organizing books by color: it would be almost impossible for you to find any books you needed. So Melvil Dewey had this realization that, if we want people to be able to use the books in the library, it makes the most sense to organize them by topic. In my apartment, that's more or less how I had them before my girlfriend rearranged them; they were organized by topic. And that was Dewey's big idea: instead of having books of the same size (or color!) next to each other, organize them by topic. That way the books that are similar are next to each other and doing research on a given subject is so much easier. So Dewey invented this numbered system that allows us to organize books by topic, and it's still the most popular system used in libraries today.

This story about Dewey made sense to the students and gave them a deeper understanding of why the Dewey Decimal system is worth learning about. A couple students came up to Kevin after class and said things like, "Did they *really* organize books like that before Dewey? That's crazy!" One student even asked for more detail on the exact meaning of each portion of the call number that was demonstrated in class.

It was, to be sure, the most interest Kevin had ever seen in the Dewey Decimal system—students actually willingly staying *after class* to hear more about hierarchies of knowledge. Evidence points to this having less to do with the inherent interest of the material and more to do with the way it was presented. By putting students in the shoes of the problem solver (in this case, Melvil Dewey), they can empathize with his plight and see the relevant problem context that he faced (as we've discussed, human beings are inherently interested in puzzles—how to organize books being one of them). In this sense, storytelling as a pedagogical approach is quite similar to narrative modeling. We still tell a basic narrative of the thoughts, intentions, and methods an individual used to solve an intellectual or practical problem, in a way that's more engaging to the human brain than straight content delivery.

Regardless of your experience or classroom persona, storytelling and narrative modeling are strong strategies for engaging student interest in the information literacy classroom. When thinking about narrative, keep this question in mind:

- Did you tie your narrative examples to a learning context of authentic expression?

Though the suggestion to "tell your students a story" sounds deeply humanistic, it has the force of scientific evidence behind it pointing to its efficacy as a pedagogical tool.

PRINCIPLE 4. ACTIVATE BACKGROUND KNOWLEDGE

A central tenet of the learner-centered approach outlined in chapter one is the importance of not viewing students as empty vessels to be filled with knowledge, but instead recognizing them as unique individuals possessing a variety of unique backgrounds and interests and a distinctively human set of cognitive capacities. Cognitive scientists have found evidence validating that what students bring into the classroom affects how they will learn the material presented during a class session. Specifically, the research has found that what we already know (or don't know) about a given topic determines how quickly we can learn other things about that topic.

What we already know about a subject, which we call background knowledge, is critical for learning new things because it helps us to make sense of the new information we are presented with and helps it to stick in our brain. Here's the basic cognitive mechanism: As discussed in chapter one, when you learn something, that information makes the transition from the working memory to the long-term memory, where it sits until you need to use it again. When you are confronted with new, related content, you either consciously or unconsciously pull that previous information out of your long-term memory and into your working memory, where it helps you decode and understand the new information. The new information and your previous knowledge are now inextricably linked, and they'll retreat into your long-term memory together, waiting until you need to use them again to apply to a relevant situation or to learn something new and related.

In essence, the research about background knowledge tells us that learning something completely new that has no relationship to anything you've encountered before is incredibly challenging. Your brain has to try to interpret it without any clues or a road map to understanding. Fortunately we can activate related background knowledge, in ways that might not seem obvious, which is why it's possible to learn brand-new skills. For example, let's say that a native English speaker who doesn't know any other language wants to learn Chinese. The two languages may not seem to have much in common. The script, the sounds, the tonalities of Chinese—they're all wildly different from English. But they are both human languages, so they do have some basic things in common (tenses, for example). A student who already knows a language with similarities to Chinese (e.g., Korean shares some characters and is also tonal) will be able to exploit her background knowledge and have an easier time than our English-speaking learner. A learner-centered teacher would help the student who knows Korean identify these points of convergence so that she has a cognitive anchor point in her brain to hang this new information on, as well as to help make sense of this new language.

Unfair as it may seem, how much we already know about a topic makes a huge difference for how much and how easily we'll be able to learn more about the topic. That's why, to maximize your students' likelihood of learning, it's important to know how much they *already* know. If you try to introduce a concept at a level too many steps beyond what students already know, they won't be able to make the cognitive connections necessary for understanding. You'll also want to help students activate their background knowledge; that is, set the stage for learning by helping them pull the knowledge they need to understand the new content back into their working memories. For these reasons, instruction needs to make concessions for both determining and building learners' background knowledge if there is any hope of moving forward.

Theory into Practice

In our example instruction request from Professor X, she asked for help in teaching students about finding good sources for their papers. But what if she'd said, "My students are required to use five peer-reviewed articles in their paper," instead? You might almost immediately hear the librarian universe letting out a hearty, collective groan. Why is this? Most (if not all) instruction librarians are cognizant of the complex information ecosystem, where peer-reviewed articles are just one possible source of reliable information. But, even more than that, we're aware that beginning research with a peer-reviewed article is simply not best cognitive strategy for novice learners. Such articles are typically narrowly focused (thus not giving a learner much of an overall understanding of the topic) and also extremely difficult to understand without advanced expertise in the subject matter. These articles are written for experts, not beginners; as such, understanding these articles without an extensive amount of background knowledge can be an overwhelming cognitive task. Indeed, asking learners who are not extremely well-versed in the subject to comprehend the language and concepts in such articles is the rough cognitive equivalent of handing the Golden State Warriors' playbook to a person who has never heard of the game of basketball and telling them, "Go play and win."

Let's think of it this way: imagine that we have a first-semester freshman taking Chemistry 101 and he's being taught by a faculty member who is a leading scholar in her field (an expert). The course employs several graduate TAs who have just completed their MSs and are now working on their PhDs. We can consider this group to be arrayed along a continuum of understanding, from someone totally new to the subject to someone with advanced expertise (see figure 3.2).

Would we think it's reasonable for the professor to talk to the first-year student about computational catalysis in the same way that she'd talk to her

FIGURE 3.2
KNOWLEDGE CONTINUUM

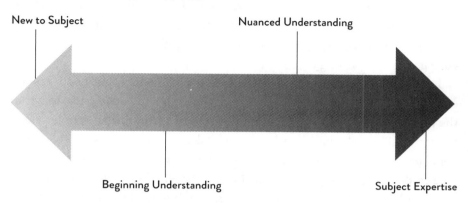

New to Subject   Nuanced Understanding

Beginning Understanding   Subject Expertise

Nobel Prize–winning colleague down the hall? We would not (we hope!), precisely because we recognize that the freshman student simply does not have the requisite background knowledge to engage with the professor as a cognitive equal in this domain. This would take many years of devoted study in the subject matter, far beyond what an introductory chemistry course at even the most prestigious institution could ever promise to deliver.

At the end of the course, the faculty member might hope that the student would have a solid, albeit cursory, understanding of some of the basic problems that chemists consider. But his knowledge would still be very far away from mastery; it would even be far away from the level of background knowledge that the TAs possess. The goal of the course is simply to advance the student along the path to mastery, while engaging with him at a level that is neither too easy nor too hard, given his background knowledge and experiences (e.g., Did he take chemistry in high school? Was it regular or AP? What subjects were covered?).

These same principles directly apply to helping students use information. If we do not believe that beginning learners have the cognitive capacity to engage in meaningful, egalitarian dialogue with experts in person (as in the case of the freshman student and the chemistry professor), there's very little reason to think they should be able to do this when engaging with expert-level published information either. We might consider published, peer-reviewed journal articles to be surrogates for the expert. Thus, as information professionals, instruction librarians must be careful not to recommend sources that extend so far past learners' background knowledge that they preclude the possibility, from a cognitive standpoint, of meaningful knowledge gains and learning.

Let's place this idea in a real-life information context, using an experience that Kevin had at the reference desk almost immediately after we wrote the preceding paragraphs, which reminded us of the importance of learners' background knowledge when helping to select information sources: A student approached the reference desk and asked Kevin for help in finding "reliable information" for her research project on whether consuming organic food was "better" than consuming nonorganic foods. The student was interested in this topic because she often found herself spending extra money on organic foods for her family on the assumption that they are more nutritious than conventional foods. The student shared her assignment, which specifically required students to obtain information on the background and history of the problem they were examining, information that supported the main thesis, and information that indicated future directions the problem might take. As they conversed, Kevin discovered that the student was writing the paper for an English-as-a-second-language (ESL) class. With this basic understanding of the learner's context, Kevin began to consider what might be appropriate background sources for this project.

The learner was at the very beginning of her research process, just starting to collect information on the topic. It made sense to Kevin to help her find sources of information that would answer basic questions like, How are organic foods defined in the United States? What is the history of thinking about organic as opposed to nonorganic foods in the United States? Is there a difference between how organic and nonorganic foods are farmed?

The student already had a good sense that these were the types of questions she needed answered and that her major information need was locating sources that would help her gather information on these issues. With a basic understanding of the student's assignment, where she was in the research process, and her background knowledge on the topic, Kevin determined that basic encyclopedia sources might be a great place for the student to expand her background knowledge. Using an online reference source through the library, the searching started very simply. Their first search term, "organic foods," helped to provide direct, reliable answers to many of the student's initial queries. This led to searches in the same resource for "organic farming," "pesticides," and several other related concepts.

This solved the immediate information need of the learner, as it gave her almost all the information she needed to complete her assignment, through a variety of detailed and reliable encyclopedia entries. At a deeper level, it also showed her how to get started with research more generally, by determining what she already knew about her topic and using appropriate background sources to build her knowledge. Kevin made sure to explain that she could use this approach whenever she was getting started on a topic, as it would help her build background knowledge, which could then lead her to further helpful information and sources. Stressing this to the student made the concept of transfer for these skills clear: using reference materials can be useful for building knowledge of any concept on any topic, not just in her current ESL class.

Indeed, for any of us who are relatively new to a topic, starting to search in this way would serve us well. We see it coming into play for learners at all levels, from recently matriculated students in community colleges to doctoral students at major research universities. For example, we often encounter researchers who assume that peer-reviewed scholarly articles are the best way to gain background knowledge on a topic. And why wouldn't they think that way, with so many assignments focused on requiring scholarly journal articles and library instruction sessions focused on finding them? Yet in many cases, learners don't have enough background knowledge on their topic to break it down into manageable research concepts that could lead to useful scholarship.

Crucially, the kinds of sources that are appropriate for a learner to use to build background knowledge will depend on the learner's current background knowledge. For example, an advanced graduate student could fairly quickly move on to relevant peer-reviewed articles after using a series of reference sources and textbook chapters to build her core knowledge of a subject. In the case of the ESL student, the reference sources that she used were both necessary and sufficient for her current information need. In fact, scholarly sources could result in a severe case of cognitive overload, by attempting to propel the learner too far, too fast along the continuum of knowledge. Indeed, out of curiosity after the student left the reference desk, Kevin searched for "organic foods" using a discovery tool and limited his search to scholarly, peer-reviewed articles. These are the actual titles of the first three articles that came up in the search:

> "Functional and Structural Characterization of Purine Nucleoside Phosphorylase from *Kluyveromyces Lactis* and Its Potential Applications in Reducing Purine Content in Food"
> "Improving the Thermostability of Acidic Pullalanase from *Bacillus naganoenisis* by Rational Design"
> "Hypoalgesia Induced by Reward Devaluation in Rats"

The rest of the articles in the search didn't appear to be much better. Initially nervous that he'd maybe not done the right thing by sending the student away with "only" reference sources (after all, he'd been trained, like many of us, that scholarly articles are the holy grail of knowledge), Kevin thus confirmed his sense that the detailed encyclopedia articles were at the appropriate level for what the student needed.

A central lesson of these case studies is that a learner's background knowledge should significantly constrain how we determine an appropriate information source at a given stage of the research process. However, a broader takeaway is that the way information is packaged can be helpful, from a cognitive standpoint, in determining how to engage learners with scholarly research. Returning to our knowledge continuum, a useful way to think about the source type a learner may find most useful at a particular stage of knowing is to consider the level of generality of the information type. For example, encyclopedia entries tend to be the most general information sources and are therefore often the most useful sources for introducing subject matter to learners at the earliest stages of knowing. Books are typically the next level of generality. Finally, scholarly articles are typically the most specific sources of information; thus, these sources may primarily be useful once learners have considerable mastery of a particular issue. These considerations, of course, are rules of thumb that will certainly have exceptions. However, as general guidelines, they offer teacher-librarians helpful practical tools for thinking about the most appropriate ways to build learners' background knowledge relative to their particular state of knowing.

In planning instruction, we find two questions related to background knowledge useful to consider:

- Where is the student in the research process?
- What does the learner already know about the topic?

The answers to these questions can go a long way toward helping us determine the appropriate sources of knowledge for learners' research.

PRINCIPLE 5. FOCUS ON DEEP STRUCTURE

In July of 2014, NBA basketball star LeBron James made a big announcement: he was leaving the Miami Heat and returning to his home state of Ohio to play for the Cleveland Cavaliers. Upon his return, James was dealing with a number of difficulties, both physical and mental.

> When James seemed scattered early last season and a former coach was asked why, he did not point to the back or the knee. He pointed to the head.
>
> "I think about a lot of s---," James agrees. "Sometimes too much. But then I try to remember what I learned from the great Pat Riley: *What is the main thing? Because the main thing has to be the main thing.*"[8]

Lebron's head was in too many places, so he wasn't focused on the thing he's supposed to be doing: *playing basketball*. Similarly, if we don't focus on the "main thing" we want students to take away from the lesson, if we do too much that doesn't have to do with the core of what we want students to learn, real learning (the kind that is retained and transferred) is much less likely to take place. That focus on the main thing leads us to our discussion of deep structure.

The concept of deep structure originates in the field of linguistics, where researchers posit that, despite syntactical and grammatical differences, some sentences share the same meaning. For example, the sentences "Dani and Kevin wrote this book" and "This book was written by Kevin and Dani" have essentially the same meaning even though they look slightly different. That meaning—what the sentence is actually about, regardless of the sentence being phrased actively or passively—is the deep structure of the sentence.

Transferring that idea to educational psychology, *deep structure* analogously means the core meanings of a practice. These are precisely the things that we want to closely pay attention to because they are transferable to new contexts. Let's return to an example from chapter one to illustrate what we mean. When discussing transfer of knowledge to a new situation, we tell a story about Kevin helping a friend load film into a type of camera he'd never seen before. If Kevin had a shallow understanding of cameras, then he would focus on the specifics of his personal Leica to identify what a camera is and how it works: for Kevin to recognize a new camera as something that he could work with, it would need to be the same color, make, and model of the camera he owns. And this would accurately describe all the silver Leica M3s in the world but not all (or even most) film cameras out there. The specifics work well for Kevin's immediate context, when he wants to take photos with his own camera, but as soon as he would encounter a new context (i.e., a different type of camera), he would be in trouble.

Fortunately for his friend, Kevin understands the deep structure of cameras; that is, how and *why* film is loaded into his camera, not just procedural knowledge, and can thus extrapolate from his experience how to approach relevant new situations. The main thing here is that all 35 mm cameras have some door that opens, some chamber where film goes, and a film leader that goes to the spool that winds the film. It's *not* the color of the camera or the side that the door opens on or any similar pieces of minutiae. Individual cameras may look radically different, but the essential components are the same. With this knowledge in mind, Kevin was able to apply critical thinking to the new scenario and successfully set his friend up to take photos with his grandma's vintage camera.

It's the *why* that really gets at the heart of deep structure and allows learners to use knowledge in novel contexts. And since one of the hallmarks of learning, as introduced in chapter one, is transfer, it is imperative that deep structure is the central focus of any effective instruction.

Theory into Practice

Demonstrating deep structure is probably the most conceptually challenging of these principles, but in many ways, information literacy lends itself to thinking about underlying meaning and structure. After all, no two research processes, even done by the same researcher, will ever look exactly the same. The question itself will differ, the search strategies will be modified, and the resources consulted will change. To that end, *everything* that we teach as information literacy specialists must be situated around deep structure; otherwise, while learners will be equipped to deal with their immediate context, they will be completely unprepared to critically apply skills to any new problem that differs in the slightest.

One of the bread-and-butter elements of library instruction has for many years been database searching. When people talk about "bibliographic instruction," this is typically what they mean. And database searching has gotten a bad rap because it is typically focused on surface-level knowledge of a database: what we like to call the *Price Is Right* style of presentation, where an instructor points out all their favorite aspects of a specific tool. But database searching is, of course, essential and unavoidable in the context of higher education research, so there must be a way to approach it that does promote significant learning.

A focus on deep structure provides that path to significant learning. Instead of focusing on what the specific filters are on a given database, instructors who focus on the underlying structure of information might spend their time talking about how keywords relate to subject terms or how information is indexed by databases or the meaning of relevancy searching, using a specific database as an example, which will have broader applications outside of the immediate context. The organization of information is the core idea behind database searching, not all the bells and whistles of the latest ProQuest product.

So, to go back to the beginning of this principle, the main thing has to be the main thing, and we need to not get distracted or caught up in other details. By narrowing down our learning outcomes for our example session, we have decided what our main things are going to be:

- feel comfortable and welcome in the library
- define an appropriately sized research question about a topic they are interested in
- develop keywords that lead them to information on their topic

Developing keywords and a search strategy can involve a number of skills and ideas, so let's break down what the deep structure of what's included in this outcome might look like. During this class session, what we are really aiming for students to understand is that keywords are the entry points for finding information on the topic they're interested in researching. When you conduct keyword searching, you're looking for that same language in the different resources that a given database is indexing, so you need to think about all the different ways that people might be talking about your topic. You'll also want to consider related concepts that might have some bearing on your topic, to provide a full picture of how that topic is viewed. An explanation like this brings the *why* of keyword generation to the surface and sets students up to think about using these same skills in the future when they need to investigate a topic in any subject.

One constant temptation when talking about keywords is to spend class time on related concepts, the most common one probably being Boolean operators. And what we (perhaps radically) suggest is that these related concepts are just *not the main thing* for introductory researchers. With Boolean operators, for example, it takes quite a long time to construct a thorough understanding of them, and it's not really necessary for first-year students. Most databases use an implicit AND when keyword searching, and it would be the unusual first-year who needed to construct such a tight search that OR and NOT were really necessary. It's not that we hate Boolean operators (in fact, Kevin spent a lot of quality time with them as a philosophy graduate student), truncation searches, wild cards, or any of the myriad other skills that are related to keywords. It's just that, for this class, right now, the main thing is learning how to develop keywords themselves and *why* they are necessary. Perhaps later on, if the opportunity arises, we can tackle these other concepts. But, for now, they are simply a distraction from the most important concept we want our learners to carry forward with them in their future research endeavors.

When planning how to approach teaching to deep structure, the following two questions can be a helpful guide for reflection:

- What is the *main thing* I want learners to walk away from this session understanding?
- What is the central meaning of the concept I am introducing, which will allow students to use this knowledge in many different contexts, not just the one we are talking about today?

These reflective questions can help keep the focus of the session tight on deep structure, or the constructs that learners will need to understand to transfer concepts to new situations.

PRINCIPLE 6.
ACTIVE LEARNING IS PRACTICE OF DEEP STRUCTURE

Active learning has been a buzzword in librarianship (and, indeed, in broader educational contexts) for several years now. Countless conference presentations have been devoted to incorporating active learning strategies into library instruction, reference interactions, online tutorials, you name it. We all agree that active learning is an important concept and critical for good teaching, but why?

In chapter one, we defined learning as "a permanent change in a person's knowledge," specifically calling out the qualities of retention and transfer. The empirical literature indicates that one of the most important ways this change takes place is through *practice*. It's not enough to hear or read or even write out a concept; for it to really stick and be applied in new situations, a person needs to actually *use* that new concept. This is the basic idea behind homework: it's an opportunity to continue *practicing* the skills that were taught in class so that the idea or procedure will lodge in the mind for future retrieval. One aspect of active learning in the classroom, then, is an opportunity for students to actually practice the skills they are being told about by their instructor.

It's not enough, though, to mindlessly perform the same action over and over again. To learn something well, a person needs to be deliberate about her practice; in the cognitive literature, this means that the individual is focused on the task at hand, is putting in effort toward getting better, has not undertaken a new task that is either too easy or too hard, and is receiving feedback from someone more expert in the domain. This is the difference between a child who becomes a concert pianist and eight-year-old Dani, who mindlessly played "Chopsticks" over and over until the kitchen timer finally rang and piano "practice" time was over.

We understand active learning, then, to be a kind of deliberative practice within the classroom setting. Providing opportunities for students to practice information literacy concepts in a meaningful way while receiving immediate and relevant feedback from an instructor is exactly why active learning is such a powerful mechanism for ensuring that they walk away from a class remembering something.

That's only half of the equation though: practice leads to retention, but it doesn't necessarily lead to being able to transfer that knowledge to a new context. That's where deep structure comes in. As we discussed in the previous principle, deep structure surfaces the underlying patterns and meaning of concepts, which is what allows for the understanding of how to use ideas in novel ways. The combination of practice and deep structure is a powerful way to provide the opportunity for student learning. Successful active learning exercises combine these two ideas.

Using active learning techniques to concretely demonstrate abstract concepts, which many information literacy concepts are, is especially potent, as cognitive scientist Daniel T. Willingham points out when he says that "the surest way to help students understand an abstraction is to expose them to many different versions of the abstraction."[9] Providing worked examples of what these ideas look like dressed in a variety of costumes, but with the underlying concepts remaining the same, can make these high-level concepts understandable to students.

Active learning is trendy for good reason: it's more engaging than a typical lecture, and the literature shows that having students practice works for getting them to remember concepts and ideas. That's pretty good, but we can take it one step further—and facilitate transfer—by explicitly planning our active learning exercises as demonstrations of deep structure.

Theory into Practice

To include both the ideas of deliberative practice and deep structure, a successful lesson plan will encourage students to engage with a concept in multiple ways, provide them with a number of worked examples they can refer to when engaging with the skill on their own, and focus on transferable concepts that apply across research contexts.

The number of potential strategies for incorporating active learning into instruction is infinite since active learning simply means that students are actively doing something other than listening to lecture. Most instructors today are likely familiar with commonly employed strategies like "think-pair-share" or the "minute paper" or using clickers to have students answer questions posed in class (more on that strategy in chapter six). For the purposes of this chapter eventually ending, we won't enumerate all the various ways that one could consider trying out active learning (there are lots of really great lists of strategies out there from various teaching and learning centers—we particularly like one from the University of Michigan).[10] Instead, we're going to focus on one example of how active learning can help students to engage with deep structure.

Let's return one final time to our hypothetical first-year writing course to consider how we can use active learning to have students practice their understanding of what keywords are and what they do. At this point in the library session, students will have already identified (at least preliminarily) a topic that they are interested in researching.

To begin, we might ask students to discuss how they typically look up information. If, for example, you wanted to find out about the newest movie starring The Rock, how and where would you look for it? What different types of things might you want to know about the film? This initial conversation (and, yes, guided discussion is absolutely active learning!) will probably lead to students talking about how they would Google something like "the rock new movie" to find out all about the movie. Then they might think about finding specific things about it, like reviews, or when and where it's playing near them, or a trailer, or how it's related to the original version of the movie (looking at you, *Jumanji*). To get to these specific things, they might add more words to their search. At this point in the class, the librarian might point out that students are essentially describing using keywords to find information and that they'll be searching in academic databases using a very similar method.

Having set the stage for what keywords are, we can now work with students on developing search terms that are relevant to their individual research topics. While there are countless ways to approach helping students actively think through creating relevant keywords, we present two options here: a linear chart and a mind-map-style graphical organizer. Of these, Kevin and Dani prefer different options, demonstrating that people can and will have personal preferences about what types of tools work best for them, but multiple tools can accomplish the same goals. One takeaway here is that a learner-centered approach can result in any number of strategies that look very similar or very different. The two most important factors to consider for any active learning strategy are that it aligns with learner-centered practices and that you feel comfortable using it.

To illustrate how both of these tools work, let's briefly return to the narrative example about Drake from principle 3. In this example, we are interested in Drake, hip-hop, and authenticity, and how those three ideas might all connect. Those ideas have been expanded into potential keywords using each tool (figures 3.3 and 3.4). Blank worksheets are available for download at www.alaeditions.org/webextras.

FIGURE 3.3
WORKED KEYWORD CHART

What is your topic, in one sentence? *How has Drake changed hip-hop?*		
Main idea #1 *Drake*	**Main idea #2** *Hip-hop*	**Main idea #3** *Authenticity*
↓	↓	↓
Specifically, what do we need to know? • Background • Biography • Life	**Specifically, what do we need to know?** • History • Credibility • Street cred • Gangster	**Specifically, what do we need to know?** • Definition • Being yourself • Credibility

FIGURE 3.4
WORKED KEYWORD MAP

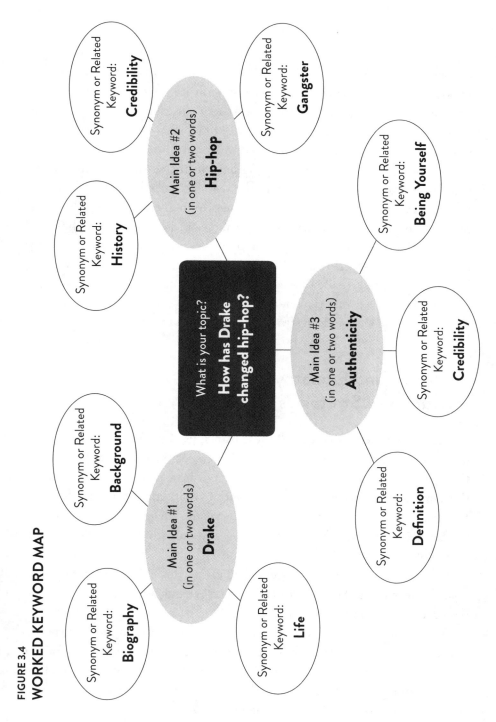

As students test these keyword combinations in an article database, they may come back and adjust, add, or remove keywords from their original list of potentially useful keywords. Emphasizing the iterative nature of designing keyword searches is a critical part of this active learning strategy. We often provide additional blank work sheets for students so that they can use the same framework as they consider different aspects of their research question.

Depending on how much time you have in the session, you might give students more or less to test out keyword searches and give them one-on-one feedback on the expansiveness or narrowness of their terminology. Providing this time to actually try out this conceptual idea in a structured way, however, is the crucial point of employing these active learning strategies. It's not that lecture in-and-of-itself is a bad thing—sometimes there are cases where a well-done lecture actually does a considerable amount of work!—but active learning provides a different modality of learning for students that allows them to experience the deep structure of concepts in action.

Evidence (and Empathy)–Based Instructional Strategies

If there is one theme that ties all these principles together, it's that the most effective instruction is designed from the perspective of the student. Effectively designed instruction takes into account how people learn and tailors the approach to maximize learning within that understanding. So even though, as we discussed at the beginning of this chapter, cognitive science sounds very clinical, it has a very strong and empathic application for the design of learning.

To help you keep all the concepts laid out in this chapter in mind, we've made a cheat sheet of the six principles to keep handy in the space where you design your lesson plans (see figure 3.5).

We've also designed a lesson-planning template for library instruction that calls for you to consider these six principles, beginning with limiting your learning outcomes and working all the way through incorporating active learning for each outcome (see figure 3.6 on page 109). This template is available for download at www.alaeditions.org/webextras.

FIGURE 3.5
COGNITIVE STRATEGIES CHEAT SHEET

Six Cognitive Principles for Organizing Information Literacy Instruction

1. Limit learning outcomes
2. Focus on a problem to solve
3. Build a narrative
4. Activate background knowledge
5. Focus on deep structure
6. Active learning is practice of deep structure

Just like any other aspect of learner-centered pedagogy that we discuss in this book, fully incorporating these best practices from the cognitive science literature will take work and practice. We hope these tools will help to get you started, and we also hope that you will be inspired to keep up with the latest discoveries in cognitive science, as they will absolutely affect our understanding of what it's like to be a person learning something.

This central idea of empathy leads us into our next chapter, where it will serve as the core for considering how we can develop meaningful relationships with our learners that can lead to improved learning outcomes.

NOTES

1. P. A. Kirschner and J. J. G. van Merriënboer, "Do Learners Really Know Best? Urban Legends in Education." *Educational Psychologist* 48, no. 3 (2013): 176.

2. H. F. Harlow, M. K. Harlow, and D. R. Meyer, "Learning Motivated by a Manipulation Drive," *Journal of Experimental Psychology* 40, no. 2 (1950): 228–34.

3. D. T. Willingham, *Why Don't Students Like School? A Cognitive Scientist Answers Questions about How the Mind Works and What It Means for the Classroom* (New York: John Wiley and Sons, 2009).

4. B. Brown, *The Power of Vulnerability*, filmed June 2010 at TEDxHouston, TED video, 20:19, www.ted.com/talks/brene_brown_on_vulnerability.

5. D. T. Willingham, *Why Don't Students Like School?*, 66–67.

6. Rosen on Drake's *Nothing Was the Same:* Is Drake the Rap-Game Taylor Swift?, www.vulture.com/2013/09/music-review-drake-nothing-was-the-same.html.

7. D. J. Arya and A. Maul, "The Role of the Scientific Discovery Narrative in Middle School Science Education: An Experimental Study," *Journal of Educational Psychology* 104, no. 4 (2012): 1022–32.

8. L. Jenkins, "LeBron's Time: Cavaliers Star Feeling the Urgency to Bring Title to Cleveland," *Sports Illustrated*, December 7, 2015, www.si.com/nba/2015/12/01/lebron-james-cleveland-cavaliers-kobe-bryant-stephen-curry-dwyane-wade.

9. Willingham, *Why Don't Students Like School?*, 88.

10. C. O'Neal and T. Pinder-Grover, "How Can You Incorporate Active Learning into Your Classroom?" Center for Research on Teaching and Learning, University of Michigan, accessed December 4, 2016, www.crlt.umich.edu/sites/default/files/resource_files/Active%20Learning%20Continuum.pdf.

FIGURE 3.6
LEARNER-CENTERED LESSON PLAN TEMPLATE

Course number/title _____

Faculty name: _____ Audience affiliation/type: _____

Venue: _____ Number of students: _____

Library instruction date/time: _____ Duration: _____

Prep time spent:

Learning Outcomes	1. 2. 3.	
Why Should Students Care?		
How Will I Connect the Lesson to Students' Previous Experiences?		

		Time
Introduction	*What is the overarching narrative of the session?*	
Learning Outcome 1	*What is my narrative?*	Time
How Will Students Practice Deep Structure?		Time

⬇ Download this worksheet at www.alaeditions.org/webextras   *(continued on reverse)*

		Time
Learning Outcome 2	*What is my narrative?*	
How Will Students Practice Deep Structure?		Time
Learning Outcome 3	*What is my narrative?*	Time
How Will Students Practice Deep Structure?		Time
Closing	*Reiterate session narrative here.*	Time
Things to Remember for Next Time		
Notes		

RELATIONSHIPS: THE HEART OF LEARNER-CENTERED PEDAGOGY

Relationships as a Catalyst for Learning

In his book *Why Don't Students Like School?* educational psychologist Daniel Willingham makes a rather startling claim: "The emotional bond between students and teacher—for better or worse—accounts for whether students learn."[1] Though this may seem fairly banal on the surface—it's not too difficult to imagine that students may tend to learn best from people they feel a connection with—the context of Willingham's statement is what strikes us as so interesting. Right in the middle of a book about cognitive principles that can help students learn (many of which were discussed in some form in the previous chapter), Willingham comes along and says that even if we do all the stuff that science tells us to do, if students don't also connect with you as a person, they're probably not going to learn a whole lot from you. We've already stated many times throughout this book that who our learners are as people matters, and we now add a further complication: the kind of person *you* are as an educator makes a big difference to learning as well.

Surprisingly, Willingham further asserts that cognitive science is of virtually no help when it comes to establishing a bond with learners. Though Willingham maintains that "effective teachers . . . are able to connect personally with students," he goes on to say, "Cognitive psychology cannot tell us how to be personable and likable to our students."[2] So although research tells us that *rapport*—the positive relationship between teacher and student—is central to effective pedagogy and learning, we need to look elsewhere to find applicable research on establishing connections with learners.[3]

Relationship Rapport and the Core Conditions of Rogerian Counseling

When planning this chapter, our first thought was to go back to the well that provided for the core of our learner-centered thinking: humanistic psychology and the pioneering work of Carl Rogers. As we discussed in the first chapter, one of the central insights of Rogerian person-centered therapy is that the relationship between the therapist and client, rather than all the facts the therapist may know about human psychology, is the most important factor in whether clients are able to move toward happiness, authenticity, and self-direction in their lives. Psychologist David J. Cain, in his book 2010 book, *Person-Centered Psychotherapies*, confirms this idea, writing,

> The quality of the therapist-client relationship almost always plays a critical role in the process of therapeutic learning. Clients are most likely to learn with and from therapists they value, like, trust, and perceive as having their best interests at heart. Conversely, clients' therapeutic progress is often impaired when they have negative or ambivalent feelings toward their therapists. Thus, a solid therapeutic relationship serves as the foundation upon which constructive learning takes place.[4]

Further research indicates that, no matter the therapeutic orientation of the counselor—Freudian, cognitive behavioral, existential, or person-centered—a caring relationship between the client and therapist is a foundational element for growth and learning.

The parallels between person-centered therapy and learner-centered pedagogy run deep, as both practices strive to facilitate significant learning, with rapport serving as an important catalyst for that learning. Whereas understanding a client's inner world to facilitate the client's autonomy and authentic mode of life defines the task of the humanistic psychotherapist, the learner-centered information literacy educator seeks to facilitate an experience where the learner explores his curiosities and passions in his approach to research. In each case, learning is deeply personal, with expressions of autonomy and the true self as a primary goal. Since both contexts have a similar deep structure of significant learning based on rapport, there is much to learn from the specific ways that humanistic counselors connect personally with their clients, which we can then apply to the information literacy context.

In Rogerian humanism, we find a general answer to the question of how a genuine connection between learner and facilitator can be established. Often, when we consider how to build rapport or be "likable" to students, there is a tendency to think that things like being funny or hip and cool are effective ways to establish such connections. However, these elements are primarily features of superficial charm and deeply variant from person to person. What one student finds funny, another might find alienating; what seems endearing to one person may seem repellant to another; and what a teacher perceives as cool might be considered by students to be a totally misguided attempt to relate on their level. And besides, we'd have an awfully hard time trying to divine what students are going to be into for every class we teach, if our intention is to use cultural or personal references to relate to learners, anyway. Learners are too diverse and interests too variable for such elements to serve as a solid psychological basis to show students that you "get them." Therefore, our best bet is to isolate universal elements of human psychology, grounded in the deep structure of *who we are as people*, that can serve as a secure emotional foundation for fostering true classroom rapport.

Drawing on Rogers and the person-centered tradition, Cain writes, "All persons have a powerful and near-universal need to be heard, seen, accepted, and appreciated as they are, including their flaws and limitations." Consequently, "the desire to hear another person as he or she shares something of personal relevance is at the heart of all good therapy and caring relationships."[5] So, from the fact that individuals desire to be their true selves and accepted for being so, we're able to make an inference about the emotional qualities we want to convey to our learners within the context of our pedagogical relationship. The way to establish an emotional bond with learners is for them to experience us as the kind of person who understands and accepts them for their authentic selves.

Empathic Understanding

Going back to chapter one, where we placed empathy at the heart of learner-centered teaching, putting ourselves in the shoes of the learner will also be a central element of our work in this chapter. A learner-centered librarian will not only possess informational and pedagogical expertise, but will also embody the qualities of a certain type of person, one who has a genuine desire to understand the inner world of another human being. Learner-centered pedagogy is the practice of empathy in action: once again, *who we are as people matters.* Therefore, as information professionals our first priority is to try to understand other individuals, and only then go on to make determinations about the specific information literacy skills these learners may need to acquire to pursue their interests.

This pedagogical practice is directly in line with the first of the three "core conditions" that the Rogerian humanistic psychologist aims to manifest in the counseling relationship, to fulfill the goal of accepting all clients for themselves.[6] This first condition, expressing *empathic understanding* of the client—and being *perceived by the person* to be an empathic individual within the context of the counseling relationship—transfers directly to the information literacy context.

Of course, a central challenge for educators interested in significant learning is discovering learners' authentic interests, goals, and passions. Rogers himself was aware of this difficulty. He wrote,

> I may be over confident . . . but I think . . . [i]f I genuinely wish
> to discover a student's interest I can do so. It might be through
> direct questions. It might be by creating a climate in which it
> is natural for interests to emerge. Although young people have
> been greatly deadened by their school experience, they do come
> to life in a healthy psychological atmosphere and are more than
> willing to share their desires.[7]

This approach to understanding learners' needs—where an information and educational need is taken to be equivalent to understanding a learner's individual interests—suggests a shift in perspective on the part of the educator and is perhaps the key place in the pedagogical relationship where we can move into a more facilitative role. Instead of viewing ourselves primarily as experts in information, our first task is to be curious about others' inner lives. In the Rogerian model of empathic understanding, true rapport requires not only understanding the nature and extent of a learner's *information* need; it also requires understanding something about the learner's needs *as a person*. To accomplish this, learners must share pedagogically relevant aspects of themselves with the librarian, which can make learners feel vulnerable.

We see this thinking in our field as far back as 1954, when academic librarian David Maxfield recognized the value of applying humanistic principles to librarian-learner interactions. Maxfield wrote that "when the inquirer is met as a unique individual, rather than as a mere consumer of bibliographical materials and techniques, his question may involve unexpected discoveries," including the "interests, goals, problems, backgrounds, and abilities of each individual student."[8] Simply adopting this empathic stance toward learners, as an opportunity to understand who they are as people, will likely improve the librarian's ability to facilitate significant learning.

In this way, transferring the first of the three core conditions of humanistic counseling psychology—empathic understanding—to the learner-centered information literacy context can be a highly effective way to build rapport. As we discussed in chapter two, the psychological research demonstrates that when human beings feel understood for who they are, they feel free to pursue their authentic selves in an autonomous way. Similarly, in the research context, when we meet our learners as individuals whom we're genuinely interested in as people, rather than merely as information problems to be solved, learners can gain the freedom to explore questions of significance to their true selves. Learners will understand that we genuinely care about them, and reference and instructional interactions will no longer be moments when librarians simply plug in information given to them by a learner, but opportunities to engage in discussions with other people about their needs, desires, and passions.

Unconditional Positive Regard

This desire to understand learners' true selves is only the first step toward effecting individuals' willingness to express themselves to librarians. Think about the people you're most inclined to share your real self with—the people, in the words of Brene Brown, you "share your truths" with.[9] We're willing to venture that you're inclined to do so because you feel safe with those people. They don't reject you, dismiss your feelings out of hand, or expect you to be other than yourself. They accept you on your own terms and provide an environment where you don't fear being emotionally vulnerable.

Similarly, Rogers posited that a central element required to establish rapport is a relationship based on acceptance rather than judgment. The psychological term for this is "unconditional positive regard," which signifies the relationship condition where individuals are able to express themselves to another person without fear of judgment and criticism. This contrasts with placing "conditions of worth" on someone, where we value them based on their conformity with our desires for their behavior. Unconditional positive regard is an autonomy-supportive, rather than controlling, emotional attitude, and when it is present in a relationship with another person, that person is likely to feel free to express genuine aspects of their personality.

Within the context of information literacy interactions, manifesting unconditional positive regard for a learner can often be as simple as explicitly articulating that research is about her as a person, and actually *meaning* it. Recall our chapter two example of the high school student researching Faulkner who challenged Kevin by saying that she was primarily interested in death. Kevin's initial intuition was that the student was, in a way, testing him. He'd already modeled for students how he would have developed an authentic topic related to *The Sound and the Fury*, but clearly she still didn't believe that the things she valued were going to be valued by an authority figure in the classroom context. Her fear, which almost everyone shares, was that if she opened up about her true self, she would be rejected. Basically, she was saying, "Okay, you want to know what I think about, Mr. I'm-all-accepting-and-anything-you-want-to-do-is-cool Librarian? *Death!* Now go ahead and be like everyone else: Tell me that's not really an appropriate thing for a 16-year-old to think about, and let's move on, hotshot!"

Instead of engaging in this expected behavior, Kevin's acceptance of the student's interest made an impact because he placed value on her unconditionally and didn't try to change her. He was, therefore, able to break through to a student who otherwise might have been difficult (she had, after all, expressed her distaste with the assignment in the first place). Kevin was ultimately able to have a serious conversation with the student, who actually paid attention to how to read a Library of Congress call number in order to find her book. The key element of this interaction, from an information literacy perspective, is that this sharing would have been far less likely had the elements of empathic understanding and unconditional positive regard not been present in their pedagogical relationship. It was rapport—the positive relationship between teacher and student—that led to learning in this context, not an objective explanation of the value of understanding how to read call numbers. In terms of measurable learning outcomes, Kevin was able to reach the same goal as if the student had inherently cared deeply about library skills (which, let's face it, is relatively rare) by engaging her sense of self.

When unconditional positive regard is present in an information literacy interaction, the librarian will have satisfied a basic psychological need, the human desire to be understood and valued. Whereas in so much of learners' educational life they are met with educators who either intentionally or unintentionally place conditions of worth on their learners via their controlling style, the librarian can make the intentional choice to meet learners with an attitude of acceptance and openness to help facilitate significant learning. The librarian can achieve this by assuring learners that the things they want to work on are worth pursuing within the context of their academic life and then helping them develop the information literacy skills needed to do so within the context of their assignment.

This skill building is important not only from the perspective of the information literacy educator, but also from the learner's point-of-view. It's simply not enough to be accepting. If we can't actually help learners locate the information they need that also feeds their interests, then our desire to help facilitate authentic learning experiences may seem to them to be empty talk. But that concrete expertise should come second to unconditional positive regard. When we make our informational expertise the first and foremost focus of our interaction, we run the real risk of missing an opportunity to facilitate significant learning. A not-insignificant number of librarians' primary objective seem to be to inform learners about all the resources and services that the library offers. While we are as excited about these things as the next librarian, without any significant, existential context to situate these resources in, we inevitably, in Maxfield's language, treat the learner as a "mere consumer of bibliographic materials" rather than a person with goals, interests, passions, troubles, and heartbreaks that have nothing to do with EBSCO databases, interlibrary loan, or the Dewey Decimal system. Connecting these informational elements to a learner's true self and need—rather than forcing learners to bend to our information demands—is a central part of manifesting unconditional positive regard in our pedagogical relationships.

Our learners can tell the difference. All human beings have a need to be heard and valued on their own merits, not as potential consumers of information. When it is clear to learners that we view them solely as the latter, we effectively place a condition of worth on them: we value you because you are a potential library user. When we recognize the dangers associated with this approach, we can instead use our informational skills as one (very important!)

element of our pedagogical relationships with learners rather than as the primary objective to demonstrate how much we know about libraries and their resources. *Who learners are as people matters* because they provide the relevant problem context for significant learning.

Congruence

The third core condition of humanistic counseling is called congruence, which we understand as being authentic and genuine in our relationships with learners. In the psychological literature, this state is often described as when what individuals are experiencing on the inside is in harmony with their outer expressions. For example, you would be congruent if you expressed joy over a Dodgers victory when you were really excited, but not if you pretended to be happy that the Dodgers lost because you were trying to impress a Yankees fan (boo). When individuals are congruent in their relationship with another person, there is a sense of emotional realness present in the relationship, which is lacking in relationships where individuals act on either an internal or external pressure to put on a facade.

The revolutionary American photographer Walker Evans spoke about his time teaching at Yale University, saying that his attitude toward students was, "I don't really know a hell of a lot more than you do except I've been around longer and I do have experience and if I can articulate it some of it will rub off and do you some good."[10] Evans was straightforward with his students about his role as a facilitator of learning rather than a "sage on the stage," positioning himself as a partner rather than an all-knowing expert. This congruence of feeling and action requires a certain amount of vulnerability, which Rogers locates as integral to learner-centered pedagogy. In "Questions I Would Ask Myself If I Were a Teacher," Rogers states that one of the central applications of humanistic counseling to education leads him to ask himself if he has the courage to risk himself emotionally in his relationships with his students: "Do I dare to let myself deal with this boy or girl as a person, as someone I respect? Do I dare reveal myself to him and let him reveal himself to me?" Though Rogers recognizes that this may be difficult—it requires courage to reveal your true self in any interaction with another person—he nevertheless concludes that "if the relationship between myself and my students was truly a relationship between persons, much would be gained[. . . .] I could step off the pedestal of the 'teacher' and become a facilitative learner among learners."[11]

Indeed, often the best learning tools we have at our disposal are simply our own experiences. The challenge is to take a risk and share them in a productive way that might be helpful to another person. For instance, a few years ago Kevin met a student who had been invited to work on a psychology research project with a faculty member while still a junior. It was a huge honor for the student but also came with pressure, so the student asked to set up a time to meet with Kevin for some research help. Kevin and the student met over coffee, and as is often his tendency when meeting with a student, he engaged the student in a discussion about his life before getting into the nitty gritty of the research project. It turned out that the student was really struggling with feelings of fraudulence. Most of the kids in his research methods class were white students who he felt "really fit in," so of course *they'd* be asked to do research! But why had this professor asked *him*—the student described himself as just a Mexican kid from the middle of nowhere—to be a research collaborator?

It was a true moment of rapport, not only because the student felt free to share a deeply vulnerable piece of himself, but also because Kevin had felt the exact same way so many times in his life. He too had felt like school was not a place for "someone like him": a "bad" kid who never seemed to fit in. These feelings of fraudulence continued, and even increased, the further he progressed in his education. Kevin not only expressed that he related to how the student felt, but also shared some of his own experiences. He talked about his high school experiences of being told to drop out of school, his feelings attending schools where the vast majority of students were wealthier, and having grown up with a single mother who worked as a waitress while attending graduate school herself.

In this case, sharing certain elements of personal experience led to congruence of emotion for both of them and helped the learner feel unconditional positive regard from the librarian after sharing challenging feelings. They discussed how they didn't have to change their innermost selves just because they were working on research in a college setting and that their backgrounds could even be an asset in imagining interesting research projects. In this way, revealing certain personal experiences helped to facilitate a significant learning interaction.

One especially noteworthy element of this example is that the learner's feeling of alienation from his educational institution stemmed from his ethnic background. Learner-centered pedagogy involves reaching all learners as people, and nowhere have we seen the relevance of relationship rapport more profoundly than with learners from marginalized groups. In their book *Existential-Humanistic Therapy*, psychologists Schneider and Krug write about applying humanistic counseling principles to their work with clients of different races from them:

> I don't believe race invariably needs to be broached between individuals of different racial backgrounds; the main issue is whether the participants can stay open to each other [. . . .] The reason for this is that it is not two races who encounter each other, but two people, and if race happens to be what is most salient at a given moment (or beckons to be addressed), then that's what should be addressed. If not, then it is a bit of a sham, and may even be more racially insensitive in itself to press the matter.[12]

Though there are many culturally relevant pedagogies popular today among contemporary librarians (which we view as completely compatible with the view of learner-centeredness outlined in this book), we think that learner-centered humanism has something unique to add to discussions of inclusion. When we meet learners as people—and manifest the three core relationship conditions outlined in this chapter in our interactions with them—we provide fruitful grounds for them to feel seen and accepted, no matter their background. And if one's background is a live, existential question for the student, we can encourage and facilitate research in these areas. So, one benefit of significant learning based on the authentic self is that it's a fundamentally inclusive approach to pedagogical problems. Who our learners are as people—their loves, their hates, their backgrounds (including race, ethnicity, sexuality, class, and gender)—are all potentially relevant significant learning dynamics in the information literacy context.

We hope to make clear that being vulnerable with a student in a learning context does not require sharing either things you deem inappropriate to share (things that would be too personal, which are hard to articulate but, like with the test for pornography, you know it when you see it), or things you feel emotionally uncomfortable with sharing (for whatever reason). In the above example, Kevin was comfortable sharing the facts about his educational life with the student, both because he felt no shame or embarrassment nor any questions about the appropriateness of the content, and also because it seemed to be, in that context, of pedagogical value to do so.

Addressing a similar point about congruence within the context of psychotherapy, Schneider and Krug set a litmus test for self-revelations based on the following principle: "The guiding therapeutic question is, To what extent does encounter build the therapeutic relationship . . . or, on the other hand, to what extent does [it] do the opposite, and defeat or stifle facilitative process?"[13] Similarly, in the information literacy context, we can ask ourselves, To what extent would revealing oneself facilitate the process of significant learning? To what extent would it hurt it?

There are certainly cases where Kevin sharing how much he hated school when he was younger could have negative pedagogical consequences. For example, if Kevin had told the eleventh-grade English student, "Look, I hated all my English class assignments and thought my teachers didn't get it when I was your age too," it could have further undermined her teacher's authority without making any gains toward significant learning in return. For this reason, Kevin didn't abandon being congruent, he just found a more pedagogically productive way to be real in the relationship with that student.

Sharing our stories and narratives with learners is not only an effective way to encourage authenticity in their own research, as we saw with the narrative modeling approach in chapter three, but it is also an effective way to build rapport by presenting as real, individual people. The contributions this can make to learning may often be subtle but have the potential to be profound.

Counselor Librarianship: Authentic Engagement in Action

Though it may seem strange to put so much focus on counseling theory in reference and instructional interactions—we're librarians, after all—the application of counseling principles and philosophy to library work actually belongs to a long but underappreciated historical tradition in information science. Maxfield, in an article published in *College and Research Libraries* over half a century ago, argues, "College librarians should give more careful attention to the individual needs of their undergraduate patrons" since "conventional reference work does not always place so much emphasis upon the library patron as an individual person as it does upon library materials and bibliographic techniques."[14] This attitude bears a remarkable resemblance to what distinguished humanistic and existentialist psychologists from the Freudian psychoanalysts who came before them. Existential psychologist Rollo May summarizes this point, writing, "What distinguishes existential psychotherapy from other types of counseling is whether the human being is an object to be analyzed or a being to be understood. Any therapist is existential to the extent that [. . .] he is still able to relate to the patient as 'one existence communicating with another.'"[15] Rather than focusing solely on the intellectual development of learners, we also care about who they are as people and about supporting their all-around personal growth. And the reason for this, according to Maxfield, is that this approach is student-centered.[16]

Counselor librarianship—Maxfield's term for this distinctive approach—was grounded squarely in the humanistic and existential psychology popular during the middle half of the twentieth century, a period during which he both worked in and wrote about libraries. Similar to the learner-centered views we've outlined in this book, Maxfield's work focused on *authentic engagement* with human beings: getting to know learners as people to help facilitate personally relevant learning. It requires librarians to understand students empathetically to help them incorporate their authentic selves into their work. In this way, according to Maxfield, we can take into account the autonomy-supportive conditions that "motivate thinking and learning and make them possible."[17]

We find Maxfield's prescience about the importance of authentic relationship rapport between librarians and learners remarkable. However, Maxfield's pioneering, deeply human work has been unfortunately overlooked by contemporary librarianship, perhaps because for so long it has been either watered down or deeply misunderstood. The need for the library educator to approach standard informational interactions, such as the reference interview, with effective communication strategies is now a commonplace understanding in librarianship. But this was not always so. In one of the leading texts on reference librarianship, *Reference and Information Services: An Introduction* (this was, in fact, the text Dani and Kevin were assigned in their reference class in library school), M. Kathleen Kern and Beth S. Woodard note that the reference interview is where "library science becomes an art" precisely because it requires librarians to not only be good searchers, but also effective at communicating with patrons.[18]

Placing the point in historical context, Kern and Woodard note that, as late as the mid-twentieth century, it was not unusual for librarian-patron interactions to be "focused more on the information needed to supply the user with resources" while ignoring "the interpersonal skills necessary to conduct the interview." This changed—at least in print—in 1954 "when David Maxfield applied interviewing principles from the counseling field to the reference interview, that acceptance, understanding, communication, and collaboration were identified as important to a successful reference interview."[19] This kind of thinking ultimately led to normative guidelines outlining best practices for interpersonal interactions during the reference interview, such as the Reference and User Services Association (RUSA) behavioral guidelines for conducting reference interactions, which stress the importance of certain personal qualities on the part of the librarian in addition to the informational skill set they possess as part of their professional expertise.[20]

This reading of Maxfield, however, underemphasizes the depth, and ultimately the radical nature, of the approach to understanding learners (and library education more generally) underlying counselor librarianship. Maxfield's central insight was not merely that successful informational transactions require effective communication. Rather, Maxfield attempted to interject into librarianship a robust *philosophy of persons* aimed at understanding users as unique individuals with a distinctive set of needs and interests because this approach not only helps them actualize as humans, but also increases their learning. He was learner-centered, as we understand it now, and his thinking was influenced by Rogers.

Expanding on Maxfield's ideas, information scientist Catherine Sheldrick Ross has prescribed conceiving of reference and instructional services as a kind of "information therapy" because, like a real therapeutic encounter in the clinical setting, it "helps a client understand their own needs."[21] In our own language of learning, the counselor librarian, like a humanistic or existential counselor, aims to facilitate a meaningful learning experience. But rather than helping learners with their personal problems, the counselor librarian's fundamental goal is to help learners be meaningfully connected to, rather than alienated from, their research.

With this context, it is important to note that our approach to building relationship rapport, as situated within the tradition of counselor librarianship, does not require us to be *therapists* for our patrons. We neither have the training for that task nor, for most of us, the interest: the counselor librarian is an information scientist to the core. Rather, as Sarah Fine recently put the point in relation to the information literacy context, "counseling is above all else a 'philosophic stance' deriving from a 'humanistic belief' in the potential of each person to be self-determining and to conduct one's life in an authentic manner."[22] That is, the counselor librarian recognizes a learners' deep psychological need to express their true selves in an autonomous way and aims to facilitate a learning experience where this is possible within the context of research. Thus, though this approach is derived from a view of person-centered therapy, it is not itself a kind of psychological therapy. For Fine, all learner-centered librarians, whether they realize it or not, are counselor librarians; it's simply a matter of whether or not we're up for the challenge:

> Librarians give people the information they need, and with it the ability to gain more control and direction in their lives. The value of counseling theory and behavioral principles is to help us do what we do better . . . We become "counselors" neither from inclination nor training, but from the inescapable weight

and intensity of our relationships. The only real question is often not whether the librarian should act as counselor, but whether the counseling is effective or not and whether it results in the right information for the right problem.[23]

There is a large body of literature—from philosophy to counseling theory to current research in educational psychology—suggesting that the right problem for librarians to focus on is facilitating the authenticity of their students, as we discussed in chapter two. The ability to establish rapport may ultimately be the most important element in determining whether we successfully help learners meet their information needs. The counselor librarian aims to help learners find a meaningful connection to their research despite the many obstacles learners may face in doing so. The learner-centered librarian is a meaning maker, helping learners avoid the potentially alienating effects of the school setting that can potentially thwart intrinsic motivation and inhibit learning. Thus, though the counselor librarian remains an information professional, he is, in a very real sense, an existential counselor as well.

NOTES

1. D. T. Willingham, *Why Don't Students Like School? A Cognitive Scientist Answers Questions about How the Mind Works and What It Means for the Classroom* (New York: John Wiley and Sons, 2009), 65.

2. Ibid., 65–66.

3. J. H. Wilson, R. G. Ryan, and J. L. Pugh, "Professor-Student Rapport Scale Predicts Student Outcomes." *Teaching of Psychology* 37 (2010): 246.

4. D. J. Cain. *Person-Centered Psychotherapies* (Washington, DC: American Psychological Association, 2010), 5.

5. Ibid., 4.

6. If you want to see these relationship conditions in action, we highly recommend watching the excellent 1965 video of Rogers conducting a short therapy session with a woman known as "Gloria." The way Rogers relates to Gloria at an interpersonal level, his warmth as she struggles with her problems, the support he offers as he guides her toward finding answers for herself, and his accepting presence as an autonomy-supportive counselor guiding his client toward self-direction—in short, how he connects with her as a person—is an invaluable lesson in authentic engagement that learner-centered librarians can learn from and adapt to their own

practices and personality styles. S. Duncan, "Carl Rogers and Gloria—Counselling (1965) Full Session," YouTube video, 45:40, posted May 14, 2003, www.youtube.com/watch?v=24d-FEptYj8.

7. C. R. Rogers, "Questions I Would Ask Myself If I Were a Teacher," *Education*, 95, no. 2 (1974): 134–39.

8. D. K. Maxfield, "Counselor Librarianship at UIC," *College and Research Libraries* 15, no. 2 (1954): 164.

9. B. Brown, *Rising Strong* (New York: Spiegel and Grau, 2015).

10. Walker Evans, oral history interview by Paul Cummings, Archives of American Art, Smithsonian Institution, October 13–December 23, 1971, excerpted in "Walker Evans on What Makes a 'Good Photograph' and Avoiding 'Too Much Pictorialism' (1971)," *ASX*, www.americansuburbx.com/2014/11/walker-evans -good-photograph.html.

11. Rogers, "Questions I Would Ask," 136.

12. K. J. Schneider and O. T. Krug, *Existential-Humanistic Therapy* (Washington, DC: American Psychological Association, 2010), 85.

13. Ibid., 85.

14. Maxfield, "Counselor Librarianship at UIC," 162.

15. R. May, *The Discovery of Being: Writings in Existential Psychology* (New York: Norton, 1983), 158.

16. D. K. Maxfield, "Counselor Librarianship: A New Departure," *Occasional papers (University of Illinois at Urbana-Champaign. Graduate School of Library Science)* no. 38 (1954): 11.

17. Maxfield, "Counselor Librarianship at UIC," 163.

18. M. K. Kern and B. S. Woodard, "The Reference Interview," in *Reference and Information Services: An Introduction*, ed. R. E. Bopp and L. C. Smith (Santa Barbara, CA: ABC-CLIO, 2011), 57–94.

19. Ibid., 57.

20. Reference and User Services Association, *Guidelines for Behavioral Performance of Reference and Information Service Providers*, revised May 28, 2013, www.ala.org/rusa/resources/guidelines/guidelinesbehavioral.

21. C. S. Ross, "The Reference Interview: Why It Needs to Be Used in Every (Well, Almost Every) Reference Transaction," *Reference and User Services Quarterly* 43, no. 1 (2003): 38–43.

22. S. Fine, "Librarians and the Art of Helping." *The Reference Librarian* 28, no. 59 (1997): 80.

23. Ibid., 90–91.

5

TRUSTING THE PROCESS
Cultivating a Growth Mindset

So far in this book, we've thought about how to get learners invested in the learning process, how to maximize our time with students in the classroom or at the reference desk, and how to build authentic relationships with patrons so that they can engage in significant learning. What happens, though, when learners encounter roadblocks on their path to learning? You can employ all the empirically validated strategies in the world, but if learners don't believe they can successfully learn and grow, those strategies won't make any difference. In this chapter, we discuss how to help students prepare for encountering setbacks and facing learning challenges since they are a natural (if not pleasant) part of research, learning, and life at large.

The Importance of Mindset

As it turns out, the way you *feel* about your ability to learn matters very much in whether you will ultimately be successful in learning something. This may come as a surprise to many; after all, most of us were brought up thinking our ability to learn is

IN THIS CHAPTER, WE

- explore how attitudes toward learning affect the ability to learn.
- connect motivation and mindset.
- situate process at the center of each and every reference and instruction interaction.

129

tied to intrinsic and inherent characteristics, like how smart we are or how quickly we pick up new ideas. With age, the aphorism "You can do anything you set your mind to!" starts to feel more and more like a lie, as you realize that your dreams of being an NBA MVP or an opera singer are unlikely to happen. And for activities and careers that rely on certain physical characteristics, that may be true. There's not a whole lot that can be done to make you taller, say, or to turn you into a soprano. But, for almost anything else that relies on learning and skill-building, the belief that you have the capability to improve and achieve matters more than any perceived quality that a person was or wasn't born with. And the best news of all is that this way of thinking can itself be taught and learned.

This concept of mindset was developed by Stanford motivational psychologist Carol Dweck in the 1990s. She and her colleagues noticed that, when presenting children with a slightly too-hard task, the kids who were eventually able to accomplish the task were the ones who professed excitement at the thought of learning something along the way and weren't deterred by the challenge of the task and lack of instantaneous success. These children's attitudes surprised Dweck and her fellow researchers and launched an entirely new field of inquiry for the psychology of motivation.

From Dweck's research, we now understand that people fall into one of two camps with regard to how they approach learning: those with a "fixed mindset" and those with a "growth mindset." Individuals with a fixed mindset believe that how much they can learn or accomplish is fixed, or limited, because of some unchangeable quality about themselves, such as how smart they are or how much talent they have in a certain area. Determining the limits of how much can be accomplished or achieved is typically very important to those with a fixed mindset so they can avoid being disappointed in themselves or feeling embarrassed in front of others. This belief can prevent people from taking an intellectual risk in trying something new or challenging and may be reinforced when a person encounters challenges or setbacks on the path to learning. The fixed mindset is a subtle and pervasive roadblock, which is why it's so important to recognize.

Let's take a very common experience as an example. Growing up, Dani was pretty good at math. In first and second grades, she was always a little bit ahead of the curriculum and especially enjoyed word problems and logic games that were like puzzles. In third grade, the school started to separate students into different math classes based on how they performed on assessments. One of the first units was geometry, a new topic for Dani. Perhaps unsurprisingly, she performed poorly on the pre-test and was placed in the back-to-basics class. "You can't be good at everything," Dani was reassured, so she concluded that she was not good at geometry. From that point forward, every time Dani was confronted by a shape, she didn't try very hard to solve the problem because she believed she was not naturally gifted in that area and could not do much about that, so she focused on other areas where she had more innate talent. Of course, shapes are pretty central to mathematics, so you could probably draw a straight line from Dani's third-grade experience to her choice to become an English major many years later.

Believing that innate qualities affect your ability to learn does, ironically enough, limit your ability to learn. That belief leads people to give up when things get tough, to engage in satisificing behavior (e.g., learning just enough to get a passing grade on the final exam but not an A), and to surround themselves with others who are also struggling with the material. It's a vicious cycle. Believing that you don't have what it takes to learn something basically ensures that it will be challenging to learn that thing.

The fixed mindset is extremely prevalent, beginning in earliest childhood when we are praised for being smart, talented, good, or other essentialist adjectives. Typically, we are conditioned to praise people this way because it feels *right* somehow, perhaps because it feels like a greater compliment to recognize natural ability. But this type of praise is insidious because it tends toward internalizing beliefs that people are either good at something or not—basically, the fixed mindset. When things go wrong, people with the fixed mindset are faced with a crisis of self-worth: getting a D on a test or burning the lasagna changes their self-perception to I'm so stupid or I'll never be good at this. And, as we've discussed, overcoming the self-image of not being good at something actually makes it much harder to improve at that task.

On the other end of the spectrum, there are some people who possess what is known as the growth mindset. These individuals acknowledge that qualities like intelligence and talent exist but that they are, at least to some degree, plastic; that is, that it is possible to change them. For instance, learners with the growth mindset typically believe that they can get smarter by investing time and energy in the area where they hope to improve. When they encounter setbacks, they start making a plan for how to improve. A person with a growth mindset dismisses the myth that intelligence is inherently fixed and believes that their abilities can be cultivated and improved through their choices, effort, and receptiveness to expert feedback.

Let's take another example. Several years ago, Dani decided she wanted to be a runner—it seemed like a nice excuse to get outside on the regular, in addition to the obvious health benefits. The day after Halloween, Dani laced up her new running sneakers, walked out of her apartment building, and proceeded to go for a run . . . of about 500 feet before she felt like she was going to die. It was a discouraging first attempt, to be sure, but Dani understood that most people are not natural-born runners. So she went home, read about twenty training plans, started running four days a week and increasing her distance slowly but surely, and two years later ran her first half marathon. Having a growth mindset about running prevented Dani from giving up after her first horrendous "run," allowed her to believe she could improve her nonexistent running abilities, and encouraged her to make a plan for that improvement.

It's important to note that, like most things in life, a single person can contain contradictions—a person might have a fixed mindset about a certain domain of learning but a growth mindset in a different area. While Dani has a fixed mindset about geometry, she also has a growth mindset about running. It's equally true that it is possible to *change* your mindset over time. In the spirit of full disclosure, that fall day when Dani finally decided to make running work was not the first time she thought it would be great to incorporate it into her life. The previous four times, she'd hit that uncomfortable wall at 500 feet, decided that she was no good at exercise, and focused on other hobbies instead. The difference came when she realized that innate talent had very little to do with being able to run (albeit slowly) and decided to commit to doing what it took to overcome the initial and ongoing challenges.

At the beginning of this chapter, we introduced the idea that the growth mindset can be learned, and now we've shown that it also can be changed.

But before we can tackle how to teach it, we need to identify the specific qualities that go into the growth mindset so we know how to approach learners in the most productive and impactful way.

The Qualities of a Growth Mindset

The growth mindset is a way of approaching learning that manifests in a number of qualities and behaviors in an individual. Teaching these behaviors through the lens of the growth mindset is important for long-term retention and transfer, as it provides the context for why the learner should care about them.

PROCESS ORIENTATION

One key difference between the fixed and growth mindsets is a focus on results over process. Individuals with a fixed mindset tend to value only the end product: Did I accomplish what I set out to do? If not, then the fixed-mindset individual considers the effort a failure. On the other hand, individuals possessing a growth mindset value the journey as much as the final result, viewing the process as an opportunity for learning and personal growth.

In fact, a growth-mindset individual may even find so much satisfaction in the road to the goal, that accomplishing the goal doesn't particularly matter. To return to our previous example, when Dani ran her first half marathon, running would be a generous way of describing what she actually did that day. After countless hours of training runs, on the big day, Dani ended up walking a lot, and her final time was about thirty minutes longer than she had hoped for. So it would have been very understandable if she'd been discouraged from running distances anymore. But Dani found value and enjoyment in all the work that led up to that day, so she decided to continue training, in hopes of doing better the next time.

As we discuss later in this chapter, the attention paid to process is one of the most crucial aspects of the growth mindset since it is highly transferable to different contexts. And since research is such a process-oriented activity, it lends itself very well to demonstrating the growth mindset in action.

PERSISTENCE

While mindset is an important factor for success in learning, skill acquisition, and improvement in our day-to-day lives, it is especially crucial to any type of creative work. There is a growing body of literature demonstrating that people who find success in creative industries, such as writers and artists, possess a growth mindset related to their work and persist in their projects, even when the going gets tough. One leading neuroscientist who studies creativity, Nancy Andreasen of the University of Iowa, found that "successful writers are like prizefighters who keep on getting hit but won't go down. They'll stick with it until it's right."[1] A persistent attitude is another hallmark of the growth mindset, allowing individuals to encounter setbacks without giving up.

One of the most famous historical examples of creative persistence is the invention of the light bulb. Though there are many apocryphal stories about Thomas Edison's development of the first commercially viable electric light, it's actually true that he and his lab tried over 6,000 prototypes before finally landing on a functional (and mass-producible) bulb.[2] While 6,000 rough drafts is a bit extreme for most people, this is a useful illustration of stick-to-it-ive-ness and the internal belief that continuing to try in the face of repeated failure (in the Edison case, *very* repeated) can result in eventual success.

In chapter one, we defined information literacy as a set of skills allowing learners to think well about what matters to them. Research, then, is an application of information literacy, where learners stitch together various information sources to construct a narrative that helps them answer their research question. (So, research could be anything from looking up the location of the nearest grocery store to finding historical information about the Civil Rights Movement, from determining if symptoms align with the flu or a common cold to designing a protocol for testing a cancer-fighting drug.) We argue that the task of research is inherently a creative act, requiring researchers to put information together and interpret it in a novel way. And, just like any other creative endeavor, research sometimes hits dead ends, requires a rethinking midway through, and stymies the most experienced practitioner. Persistence in the face of adversity is key for researchers as much as it is for artists and inventors.

GRIT

When talking about mindset, one concept that frequently gets brought up is grit. In their seminal 2007 article, researchers Duckworth, Peterson, Matthews, and Kelly define grit as "perseverance and passion for long-term goals."[3] Grit gets at the idea that intrinsic motivation (which we discussed in chapter two) is a crucial component for learners to stick with difficult learning experiences, especially over a long period of time. Grit certainly has an element of persistence, but the underlying motivational framework is an interest in the topic to be learned, leading to the determination to do whatever it takes to accomplish the learning goal.

One of the most interesting aspects of grit is that it has been empirically demonstrated to be separate from innate intelligence. This observation further amplifies the central message of the growth mindset—that innate ability will only take you so far—and that it is possible to change one's ability in a certain domain over time.

Interestingly, a recent meta-analysis of the grit literature found that the conception of grit alone had limited impact on performance and most of that impact was due to persistence (though interest did also play a smaller role).[4] Despite this finding that the complex concept of grit may not have the outsize impact that earlier researchers hypothesized, we still think it's a useful concept for tying learner autonomy and motivation together.

Before continuing on to applications of the growth mindset in the library and information literacy contexts, we want to acknowledge the number of critiques of the growth mindset and associated motivational theories. A significant body of criticism claims that teachers employing a growth-mindset pedagogy are telling students to simply "work harder" and that this disproportionately affects students from disadvantaged backgrounds. These critics specifically call out mindset theory's emphasis on the individual as problematic since many of the inequalities in our educational system are institutional and systemic. They worry that the individual focus may shift the responsibility for student failure back onto students, without addressing the larger inequalities at play.

Carol Dweck herself has responded to these criticisms, with most of her comments boiling down to educators needing to be careful about how they apply ideas from her theory.[5] For example, while mindset theory does emphasize that hard work and persistence are important for improvement, this is only a single piece of the mindset puzzle. Just like learner-centered pedagogy more broadly, employing a growth-mindset framework in teaching takes commitment. Simply adopting the work-harder aspect of growth mindset might cause more harm than good to students, who may internalize the wrong message, such as, I am working as hard as I can, but I don't seem to be improving; therefore, I must not be smart after all. But a comprehensive approach to growth mindset—including an emphasis on hard work as well as persistence, acknowledgment that intelligence is not a static quality, consistent and meaningful feedback, and a focus on process—*can* lead to the outcomes promised by mindset theory. In fact, when mindset theory is fully and appropriately implemented in a classroom, students who have the most academic challenges tend to demonstrate the most significant improvement.

So, with this explicit acknowledgment that there's more to the successful implementation of mindset theory than in the popular understanding, let's consider how we can help cultivate a growth mindset in our library learners.

The Growth Mindset in the Library Setting

If your library is anything like the libraries that we've worked in, then on any given day a student will approach the reference desk to ask for help, prefacing her request with something like, "I'm just not good at research" or "I'm bad at this library stuff." These students are brave in deciding to and ask for help (which is a huge hurdle to overcome), so we might reasonably assume that at least an equal number of people have the same I'm-bad-at-this attitude and *don't* ever ask a reference librarian for assistance. And what these preliminary phrases indicate to us is that many, many people have a fixed mindset when it comes to research; they don't tell us that "research is challenging," but rather the self-reflective and self-defeating "I'm not good at this." A primary goal of library educators must be to create the conditions and self-image for learners to believe that they can improve their research skills—that it is within their realm of control and ability.

Several pages ago, we discussed that one of the critical qualities of a person with the growth mindset is a focus on process. Research, it is commonly understood, is itself a process. Typically, one must take several discrete steps to arrive at a conclusion to a research question, though the precise steps will depend on the question being asked. By making process central to both our instruction and reference interactions, we can help learners focus on process as a natural part of their approach to research.

Let's briefly return to our running example to illustrate the importance of the focus on process. When Dani started running, she knew that she really wanted to run a half marathon, a relatively arbitrary distance that has taken on major symbolic meaning for many a casual runner. At first, she could barely run at all. But in a few weeks she could run five kilometers without stopping (or, at least, too much). That being said, a month in, there was no way Dani could run a half marathon. This didn't make her a failure though—it meant that she was on the path to that end and should give herself a lot of credit for having put in the work to get to that point. It's all a matter of perspective: If she had tried to run a half marathon a month into her training, yes, she would have "failed." But if she viewed the month's progress as a part of the journey *toward* a half marathon, then she was definitely doing all right, even though adding each mile would continue to be challenging.

Research works in much the same way. You might not be able to get the final result (i.e., the complete research paper) on the first day, but that doesn't mean you are failing somehow. You might have made progress on defining your research question, taking a first go at developing a search strategy, or any number of aspects of the research process. And you might continue to make progress very well for a while before hitting a wall at another point in the process—which doesn't make you a failure either. The growth-mindset concept tells us there is a way past these roadblocks, through persistence and effort. But seeing each discrete piece of research simply as part of a larger whole is critical because it helps to prevent those feelings of failure—yes, this part is tough, but look at how far you've come.

This focus on process is a fruitful way to spend one's reference or instruction time since the research process *is* something that transfers well between domains. Whether a student is writing an essay for a literature class or designing an experiment for her neuroscience lab, she will still go through the same basic iterative steps.

Consider our student at the reference desk who arrives with a low self-image of his research ability. "I'm writing a paper on the American Dream," he says. "But I just can't find any articles on my topic. I'm not very good at this research thing."

The first thing that probably goes through a librarian's head is, Holy smokes! The American Dream is a big topic, and I'm sure there are basically infinite resources out there about it. But of course that's not what she *says* to the student. Instead, the librarian starts out the reference interaction with a learner-centered reference interview, focused on the student's background and interest, as outlined in chapter two. After figuring out more precisely what this student will need for his assignment, the librarian will start to help him find resources. This is the moment when the librarian can really start to incorporate growth-mindset theory and focus on research as process.

First, the librarian would work with the student to generate a set of keywords. "This is our first pass at creating these search terms," she might say. "We might imagine and find more specific or different keywords once we start searching and see the type of language other people use to talk about the American Dream. We don't have to get our list perfect right now; we just need enough to get started."

At this point, the librarian and the student would start searching, most likely in a relatively broad database like Academic Search Complete. The librarian would explain why they are starting with a discipline-agnostic tool like this and that they may decide to use a different tool later in the process as they start to uncover what disciplines are most interested in the American Dream (perhaps history, perhaps sociology, perhaps something else). After running a purposely broad search, like "American Dream," they would discuss how to start narrowing things down from the 57,000 items retrieved to what the student is specifically interested in. Together, the student and the librarian might run two or three different searches, to see how the results change. "Notice how we are finding different potentially useful things in each of these searches," the librarian might say. "So it might take a number of different tries to find the right combination of words and resources."

During the reference interaction, some of the searches might come up with null result sets or a list of articles that are completely irrelevant. Positioned as an expert in research, the librarian must be vulnerable and explain, for example, why they hit a dead end or how they made a mistake. This sets up the expectation for the student that these things are *normal* and not reflective of some deep-seated failure.

Once the student has a search strategy and has identified a few articles to get started, he will most likely be ready to conclude the reference interaction. At that point, it's critical for the librarian to reaffirm that while the student might not find that one perfect source right away (or indeed ever), he will almost always be able to find sources that speak to some piece of his topic. This may require breaking the topic down into different parts to search for and then piecing those parts back together to make a new argument, or it may take a number of different search strategies in different search tools, but he *will* be able to make it work. Research is a process and a learned skill, so if he keeps working on it, he will get better.

One concluding question both Kevin and Dani have encountered at the end of a reference interaction like this is, "Where did you learn how to do all of this?" And, while of course we acknowledge that we went to library school, we really focus on it taking a lot of years and trial and error to learn the ins and outs of breaking down research questions and searching. Basically, the major difference between us and the student is that we've gone through this process many, many more times. This question is a terrific setup for breaking down the expert-novice barrier, exposing that research skill can be changed (i.e., we weren't born being super researchers!).

While interactions at the reference desk may provide many opportunities for focusing on process and the growth mindset, in many ways, demonstrating process in an information literacy session can provide more options for the instructor: you can take more time to focus on process *before* the students even embark on their project for the course, and you can also use the opportunity for students to engage in active learning with one another. In addition to exposing the deep structure of research, these activities can be an opportunity for students to see that they are not alone in their thoughts and feelings about research.

For the past several years, whenever Dani works with an introductory writing class, she guides them through an exercise to map the research process.

This activity came into being after Dani noticed, over and over again, when it was time for students in the instruction session to conduct their own research, they would raise their hands and say, "There isn't anything on my topic. Should I choose a new topic?" It became clear to her that many students did not have a sense of research as a process, let alone a creative process. They expected to enter their keywords, find an article that answered their research question (the myth of the "one perfect source"), and then write their paper. So, it seemed increasingly important to devote time to the idea of process.

Dani starts the exercise by asking how many students have written research papers before: If very few have, then the class will begin by mapping writing a paper and will add in the research component afterward. Otherwise, they dive right into the idea of research. Depending on the class size and how much time she can devote to the exercise, Dani may either have the students work in small groups or as a class. She provides the start and end points for the map ("Receive the research paper assignment" and "Turn in the research paper assignment," respectively), but everything else is up to the students to provide.

> "What is the very, very first thing you do when you get a new assignment?" Dani asks the students, to get them started on the map. Almost invariably, someone will say, "Read it!"
>
> "That's an excellent way to start," Dani says.
>
> "What should we put next?" someone else asks.
>
> "Whatever it is that you personally do next," Dani responds. "Your process is going to be personal to you, so no two maps are going to look exactly the same."

This exercise has provided a huge range of interesting maps that surface pre-conceived notions about research, as well as find common ground with other students in the iterative, and sometimes frustrating, nature of the research process. One of the best compliments Dani has received from a faculty member came after one of these sessions, when he said, "I had no idea that my students thought about research that way," and then proceeded to rewrite his assignment for the following year with a more explicit focus on process (such as including required check-ins at certain points before the paper was due).

FIGURE 5.1
WORKED RESEARCH PROCESS MAP

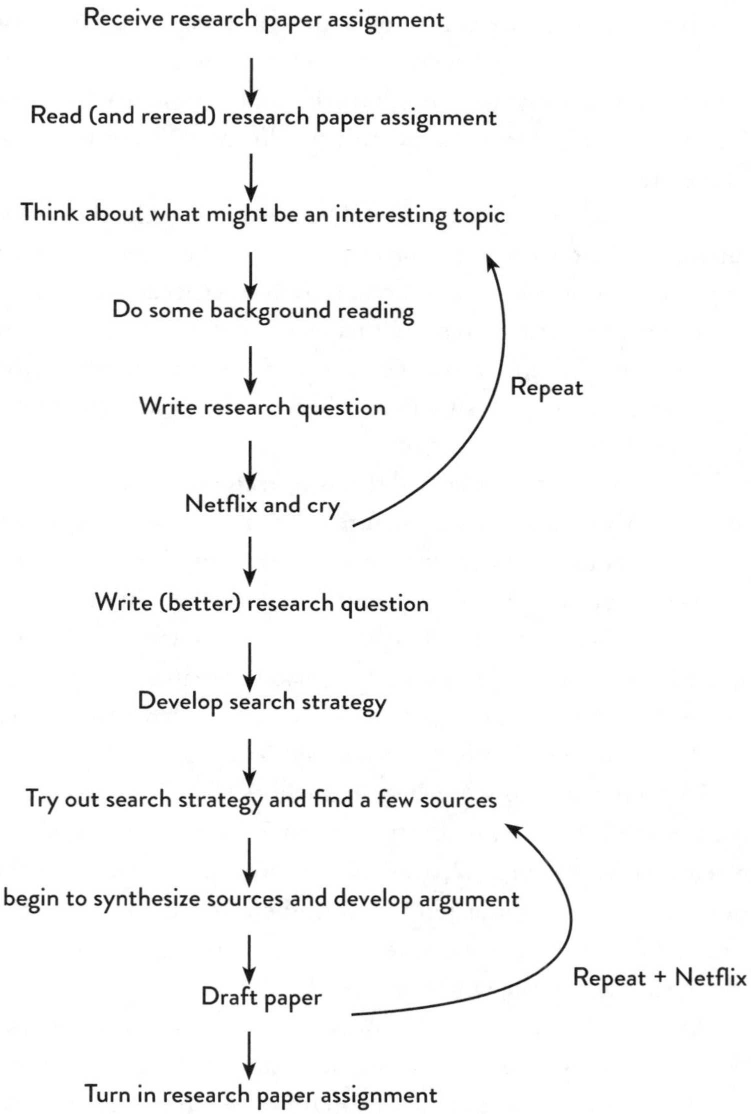

Receive research paper assignment

↓

Read (and reread) research paper assignment

↓

Think about what might be an interesting topic

↓

Do some background reading

↓

Write research question

Repeat

↓

Netflix and cry

↓

Write (better) research question

↓

Develop search strategy

↓

Try out search strategy and find a few sources

↓

begin to synthesize sources and develop argument

↓

Draft paper

Repeat + Netflix

↓

Turn in research paper assignment

As you can see from the sample completed research-process map in figure 5.1 (which is based on a real map Dani did with a first-year English class), the students began to recognize that parts of the process repeat over and over again throughout the course of writing a research paper (not only "Netflix and cry" but "develop keywords"). This demonstrates how messy research can be and that it will require practice and persistence to get to a successful outcome. (A blank map is available for download from www.alaeditions.org/webextras.)

This mapping exercise is useful because it helps learners to recognize and identify their own research process, without the library instructor determining what that process is for them. However, especially for students who have no experience writing research papers, the mapping exercise itself can be a bit daunting. In those cases, it can be useful to lead students through a sample research process but ask them to reflect on the various elements and activities contained within it.

One way we've approached this is by using worksheets that ask students to consider their process to structure a library instruction session. These tools also have additional benefits: they could be used for students to do pre- or post-work around the session, and they could be shared with a faculty member who wants his students to get reacquainted with the research process but can't bring them to the library for whatever reason. So, while the worksheet we include here was designed to be a tool for synchronous learning, it can easily be adapted to asynchronous contexts.

Using the process worksheet in the library session, the instructor discusses each section before giving students time to work through the exercises on their own (see figure 5.2, available for download from www.alaeditions.org/webextras). After about ten minutes, the class comes back together and the students share their experiences and thoughts before the class moves on to the next piece of the worksheet.

As you can see from the worksheet, in some ways the research process is presented as falsely linear, by necessity of the format. One of the most important things the instructor can do while providing context for each section is remind students that it's unlikely their process will be as straightforward and clear as the worksheet lays out. Some sections may need to be

FIGURE 5.2
BLANK PROCESS WORKSHEET

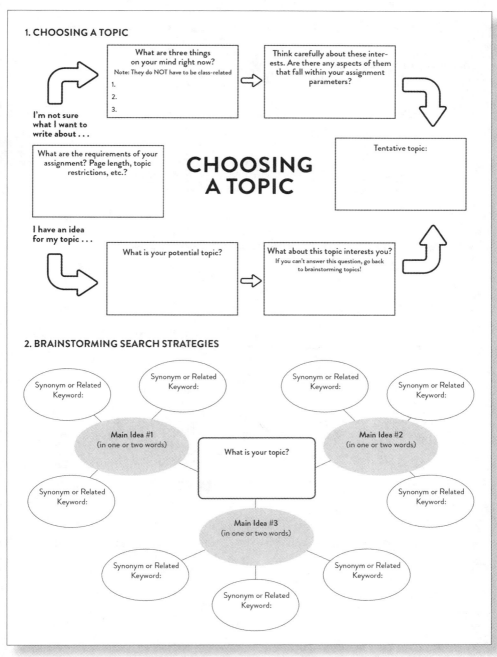

1. CHOOSING A TOPIC

I'm not sure what I want to write about . . .

What are three things on your mind right now?
Note: They do NOT have to be class-related
1.
2.
3.

Think carefully about these interests. Are there any aspects of them that fall within your assignment parameters?

What are the requirements of your assignment? Page length, topic restrictions, etc.?

CHOOSING A TOPIC

Tentative topic:

I have an idea for my topic . . .

What is your potential topic?

What about this topic interests you?
If you can't answer this question, go back to brainstorming topics!

2. BRAINSTORMING SEARCH STRATEGIES

Synonym or Related Keyword:

Synonym or Related Keyword:

Synonym or Related Keyword:

Synonym or Related Keyword:

Main Idea #1 (in one or two words)

Main Idea #2 (in one or two words)

What is your topic?

Synonym or Related Keyword:

Synonym or Related Keyword:

Main Idea #3 (in one or two words)

Synonym or Related Keyword:

Synonym or Related Keyword:

Synonym or Related Keyword:

⬇ Download this worksheet at **www.alastore.ala.org**

(continued on reverse)

3. FINDING RESOURCES ON YOUR TOPIC

Using a general library database, try out a search for your topic using the search terms you brainstormed in Part 2.

What keywords did you use to search?

How many results did you get? Does that seem like more than you expected? Less?

What is the first resource that shows up in the search? Does it seem relevant to your research interest?

Are there any resources on the first page of results that look promising to you? Write down the titles here.

4. MODIFYING YOUR SEARCH

Now change your search up—you could choose to try totally new keywords from your original brainstorming, different combinations of words, or adding another search term to your original search.

How did you change your search?

How many results did you get? Is that more or less than last time? What might be the reason for that change?

What is the first resource that shows up in the search? Does it seem more or less relevant to your research interest than the last first result?

Are there any resources on the first page of results that look promising to you? Write down the titles here.

144

even if you are an expert. Seeing this messiness in action, with the help and support of a librarian who can confirm that it is a good and natural thing, can be a powerful way for students to get past a roadblock in their process.

Finally, we would be remiss in writing a chapter about mindset if we didn't specifically talk about praise. Often if people know one thing about mindset theory, it's that the type of praise you offer matters. Growth-mindset praise specifically "praise[s] the process, not the person."[6] In other words, as a person of authority (the instructor-librarian), you want to praise things an individual has control over, not essentialist characteristics (e.g., intelligence, talent). Just like the example classroom exercises we provided above, praise can change the learners' focus, from what they feel they are coming into their research with, to what they may be able to walk away with from this experience. The concept of process continues to be central to everything related to mindset theory. To illustrate, here are some examples of what process praise might look like in a library setting:

- "You worked hard on developing that list of keywords, and it really paid off in the interesting and precise searches you were able to construct."
- "I know it wasn't easy to narrow down your topic, but specifically breaking it down into constituent parts and then selecting the piece that remained most relevant to you made your research question much stronger."
- "I'm impressed by how you kept trying different combinations of search terms in different databases until you found a combination that worked for you."

Notice that none of these examples says anything about being smart, a good student, or even good at research (even if the student may well be!). Instead, the praise focuses on the work that they put in to get to the end result, which may not be a perfect one. But it demonstrates that the work *matters* and that students have agency in improving their research performance.

The Growth Mindset in Everyday Practice

It would be disingenuous to say that the only people who can benefit from a growth mindset are the those we encounter in our reference and instruction interactions. Indeed, as educators we learn more about ourselves and our teaching every day, and one of the most impactful ways that we can do this is to apply a growth mindset to our own practice. Changing what you do in the classroom or at the reference desk is not easy, and we recognize that. You don't flip a switch one day and suddenly embody all the things we talk about in this book. (Full disclosure: neither one of us does either! But we work a little, every day, toward that goal.) So, you might start with taking a growth-mindset approach when applying ideas from this mindset to your work. Recognize that it is a process, and you will make progress, but some days you might take steps backward as well.

Let's take praise as an example. It is *not* easy to offer process-oriented praise on the fly. It's pretty easy to say "good job," but growth-mindset praise begs for specifics to be successful. Don't beat yourself up for telling students that they are good at research, so long as you are conscientiously trying to help students focus on process overall and the idea that they can always improve their natural-born talents.

To that end, here are a few questions for reflection, which encourage you to consider how you are working to incorporate a growth mindset (and, indeed, learner-centered pedagogy more broadly) into your librarianship practice:

- In working with a learner, did I focus my feedback more on process instead of the end result?
- Did I explicitly remind learners that they are capable of improvement and that their skills are not fixed?
- Did I try to praise the work, persistence, and process of learners instead of their inherent qualities?

If you work toward a *yes* to these questions, then you are working on cultivating a growth mindset in your learners.

NOTES

1. Nancy Andreasen, "The Relationship Between Creativity and Mood Disorders," *Dialogues in Clinical Neuroscience* 10, no. 2 (2008): 251–55, quoted in J. Lehrer, "Depression's Upside," *The New York Times*, February 25, 2010, www.nytimes.com/2010/02/28/magazine/28depression-t.html.

2. J. Latson, "How Edison Invented the Light Bulb—And Lots of Myths About Himself," *Time.com, Technology* (blog), October 21, 2014, www.time.com/3517011/thomas-edison/.

3. A. L. Duckworth, C. Peterson, M. D. Matthews, and D. R. Kelly, "Grit: Perseverance and Passion for Long-Term Goals," *Journal of Personality and Social Psychology* 92, no. 6 (2007): 1087–101.

4. M. Credé, M. C. Tynan, and P. D. Harms, "Much Ado About Grit: A Meta-Analytic Synthesis of the Grit Literature," *Journal of Personality and Social Psychology*, published electronically June 16, 2016, doi: 10.1037/pspp0000102.

5. "Teachers, Parents Often Misuse Growth Mindset Research, Carol Dweck Says," Hechinger Report, *USNews.com*, November 23, 2015, www.usnews.com/news/articles/2015/11/23/teachers-parents-often-misuse-growth-mindset-research-carol-dweck-says.

6. Mindset Kit, "Praise the Process, Not the Person," accessed November 15, 2016, www.mindsetkit.org/topics/praise-process-not-person.

THE LEARNER-CENTERED TECHNOLOGIST

What about Technology?!

At this point, you may have noticed that we've gone pretty far into this book with relatively few mentions of technology. Apart from a few hand waves toward online research guides, we haven't focused on this aspect of contemporary higher education life, something that consumes many hours of a teaching librarian's working (and nonworking) time. Why is that? Do learner-centered pedagogy's roots in humanistic psychology and philosophy make it too old school to apply to the high-tech environments of today's libraries? Can we imagine a learner-centered approach to librarianship that deeply engages with digital tools?

Our answer to the last question is a firm yes—while the learner-centered librarian will look at each new technology that comes into vogue with a wry eye, there is certainly room to incorporate novel approaches into our practice. We've saved our discussion of technology for the last chapter to build a solid foundation in the theory and key tools of learner-centered practice without

IN THIS CHAPTER, WE

- situate learner-centered librarianship within the digital realm.

- propose a learner-centered approach to selecting class-room and library technologies.

- suggest strategies for thoughtfully incorporating technologies into teaching.

getting distracted by specific (and ever-changing) technologies. Now that we have established a baseline set of values and practices, we turn to applying them to the domain of technology: transfer in action!

When planning out this book, we decided to address the use of technology in its own chapter, for a few reasons: First, across the profession (but this is by no means unique to librarianship), there is a lot of fetishization as well as anxiety around technology. And there is significant polarization—there are large groups who think technology will either save the profession or end it. We view technology as a means to an end, but not an end in and of itself. In this chapter, we won't come down on either side of this debate, but rather provide a framework for evaluating the use of individual technologies as a learner-centered library practitioner.

Second, we understand that there are external pressures to incorporate technology into our work. Most of this is well-intentioned, with the idea that adding tech to our work will make things more efficient and effective and will prevent the profession from being left behind. The framework we present in this chapter is meant to provide you with the confidence to say, "Yes, absolutely, this technology can help me do my job better," or "No, thank you, this technology does not align with my learner-centered approach that I can demonstrate leads to significant learning."

We want to be clear that being learner-centered does not mean being antitechnology (in fact, let's all take a moment to ponder that time Dani talked her boss into being an early adopter of Google Glass); it just means applying the same critical eye to technology that we apply to any other practice. Just as we've evaluated methods of teaching throughout this book by looking at what the evidence in the literature tells us, we want to use the same methodology of employing evidence to justify our decisions to use various technologies in library work.

So yes, we can imagine a learner-centered library instructor who teaches in a completely online environment or a librarian who designs digital and analog tools to enhance an in-person session or even one who pulls out a variety of nifty technological gadgets for students to engage with during their one-shot library session. It all depends on the underlying reasons for employing a specific tool or technology and whether it ultimately enhances the learning experience.

What *Is* Technology?

As always, before we start digging deep into our subject, we want to ensure a common understanding of the terms we're using. So, although what we mean by technology may seem obvious, we think it's fruitful to pause for a moment and define precisely what we mean by technology.

Typically, when we talk about technology as a profession, we are referring to high technology, involving computers or electronics in some way. And while we use computer-based tools for many of our examples in this chapter, it covers a very broad view of technology. One definition of technology that we find useful is "a system that uses knowledge and organization to produce objects and techniques for the attainment [of] specific goals."[1] What's great about this definition is that it is encompassing—any tool or strategy that you use could be considered technology. Basically, technology is anything that is not just you talking to learners. Whether you are having students work through a printed handout or are creating an immersive library experience through a virtual reality headset, it's all technology, and it all needs to go through the same scrupulous vetting process we describe in this chapter.

Throughout the book, one implicit assumption we've held is that, all other things being equal, creating a person-to-person connection via discussion and interaction with students is the default mode for learner-centered teaching. After all, if the heart of learner-centered pedagogy is relationships, anything that puts up the slightest barrier between the instructor and the learner must prove its value in order to be utilized. We hold these tools to a high standard because creating relationships is extremely important. But there are many scenarios where using a given technology does allow for increased attention to other parts of the learner-centered mix, such as autonomy or motivation.

Looking back to chapter two, let's consider the topic-selection flowchart worksheet that Dani created based on Kevin's master's paper research. It's not a particularly complicated handout, but we still consider it technology since it is not just the librarian having a conversation with students and is a specific tool created for a specific purpose (i.e., helping students choose a topic that is meaningful to them).

As you'll see in the next section, Dani created this worksheet because it was learner-centered in nature. It took something learner-centered that Kevin was already doing (helping students exercise their autonomy by selecting interesting topics to research) and transformed it into a physical object that allowed for a different set of affordances. We revisit this example because we think it's helpful to think about something seemingly so simple—a printed handout—and put it through a rigorous set of criteria before adopting it into our practice.

In the next section, we propose a set of specific questions to help determine if the use of a specific technology aligns with the learner-centered principles we've laid out in the previous chapters.

A Framework for Incorporating Technology into Learner-Centered Practice

We live in an age of invention, and new tools for teaching, learning, reference, cataloging, customer service, and a multitude of other library-related functions enter the market every day. It can be very exciting to encounter tools that promise to make our lives easier and help us do our jobs better, but it's also sometimes overwhelming to determine if these tools can live up to their claims. While we can't really help you determine if a technology is "good" or if it's worth the hassle or expense (that's an individual judgment call), in this section we explain how to determine if it has the possibility of being used in a learner-centered way.

Notice that we say "used in a learner-centered way." We've phrased it this way because we'll examine each technology based on two criteria: the inherent capabilities of the tool and the way it is used in the library setting. Some technologies have structural issues that would make it extremely hard, if not impossible, to use in a learner-centered way. For example, an application that relies on Flash to operate would fail the learner-centered test because the Flash Player is not available on all devices an individual student might use. In most cases, however, it is the implementation of the technology that determines whether it might be considered learner-centered.

Next, we propose three questions for the learner-centered practitioner to apply when making decisions about using technology in professional practice. These questions are presented in the order we suggest evaluating the technology: that is, if the answer is no at any point, that is strong cause for dismissing the technology, beginning with question 1. We explain how these questions get at learner-centeredness, and at the end of this section you'll find a handy flowchart that summarizes this decision-making framework (figure 6.1).

QUESTION 1. DOES THIS TECHNOLOGY ALLOW ME TO DO SOMETHING THAT I WOULDN'T BE ABLE TO DO OTHERWISE?

Before considering anything else, we need to evaluate why we are interested in a given technology for our practice. Are we adding technology for its own sake or because it will allow us to do something that we wouldn't be able to otherwise? This might mean doing something better or doing something completely new.

Another way to think about this is, What problem is this technology helping me to solve? Examples of common challenges in library instruction that technology may help mediate include large classes, students in a variety of physical locations, the "one-shot" library session, and assessment. Notice that we say "may" here—success will depend on the implementation and affordances of the individual tool. There's pretty much nothing that comes right out of the box that can solve an instructional problem without a little bit of creative thinking on the part of the librarian.

But before you start thinking, What technology should I use here?, we'll want to consider the problem context to determine if incorporating technological tools is appropriate, or simply a distraction. For example, if the problem is about helping students to understand academic honesty, there are practically infinite ways to approach it. And if your current tech-free teaching method does an excellent job of achieving learning goals, there may be no reason to change it. But in a case where your current strategy is not achieving the desired results, or you need to introduce a new element (e.g., you need to assess one thousand freshmen on their understanding of plagiarism), there may be a call for considering technology as a possible solution.

One thing to keep in mind is that there's usually both a no-tech/low-tech solution and a high-tech one, so it is going to be up to your comfort level and needs to decide which route you want to go. Let's go back to our brief academic-honesty example. In a scenario where you need to evaluate learners' understanding of plagiarism in a comprehensive way, you could either provide an evaluation mechanism on pen and paper, by capturing student discussion, or through quizzing software. Depending on the type and complexity of the evaluation you want to perform, the software option might be a clear winner—it allows you to grade student work on predefined answers almost instantaneously, can provide (canned) feedback to students, and gives the librarian back some precious time—or the pen and paper option might be the better choice, especially if you are looking for evidence of higher-order thinking in a free response. It's a balancing act between what a tool allows you to do and what you might lose by any sort of mediated instruction.

Let's return to our research topic worksheet example from the beginning of this chapter. The problem at hand is demonstrating to learners how to choose a topic that is meaningful to them for their research project. You could absolutely use a narrative to demonstrate it, but it can be challenging for students to visualize the process as a process without a step-by-step map. The worksheet helps students imagine a working mental model of the topic-selection process and invites them to place themselves in the center of the process. This accomplishes something that discussion by itself would probably not, by clearly visually representing the process. This being the case, it clearly passes our first test since this lo-fi technology allows us to do something we couldn't do through direct instruction alone.

Incorporating any new technology into your teaching takes work. First, you must learn how to use the technology. Then, once you understand how the tool works, you need to consider how best to use it in your practice, whether that's adjusting something you are already doing to incorporate the new tool or inventing a whole new way of doing something. Finally, you test how the tool works in your context and make any adjustments (or even abandon the tool if it's not working the way you intended) along the way. It's not a controversial statement to say that time is one of the most precious resources of any library practitioner, and even if you select free tools to work with, there is a cognitive cost. So before you try out a new tool, you'll want to weigh whether it's helping you achieve authentic learning in a more significant way.

QUESTION 2. CAN THIS TECHNOLOGY AID ME IN CREATING A MORE LEARNER-CENTERED EXPERIENCE?

This is the core fundamental question for library practitioners to consider when evaluating technology: Does this technology allow me to enhance my learner-centered practice in some way? This might mean engaging with any of the concepts previously discussed in this book, ranging from cognitive engagement via active learning to the creation of a more inclusive and welcoming learning environment. There are many ways to understand "learner-centered" in a practical context.

This question asks you to think about what specifically you might be interested in using the tool for in your teaching, and how it might contribute to significant learning, as defined in chapter one. What can this tool or strategy do for you in terms of supporting retention, transfer, autonomy, motivation, mindset, or inclusiveness? Conversely, what does the technology limit you in being able to do?

As we've seen throughout the course of this book, learner centeredness has many components and can take a wide variety of forms. To help illustrate the variety of factors that can go into consideration of this question, below we provide a (non-exhaustive) list of sub-questions you might consider in determining whether a given technology creates a more learner-centered experience.[2]

- Does the technology contribute to significant learning as we defined it in chapter one?
- Does the technology help emphasize learners' personal interests and help them to see themselves in the course content?
- Does the technology facilitate students' exercising autonomy in their learning?
- Can the technology allow students to build relationships with one another?
- Does the technology provide additional opportunities for demonstration or practice of deep structure?
- Can the technology be used to help students learn at their own pace?

Let's turn again to our research topic selection worksheet. It's based on the learner-centered concept of picking a research topic of personal and authentic interest. The worksheet's flowchart helps students think through this process, which is specifically designed with significant learning in mind and engages deeply with autonomy-supportive pedagogy by inviting students to place themselves in the center of the process. Thus, it absolutely meets the criteria for helping to create a more learner-centered environment.

We would examine any other technology, tool, or strategy in the same way. If it meets the fundamental criteria of directly supporting significant learning, then we would consider it to be learner-centered. It doesn't have to do all the things we've laid out in this book as learner-centered, it just needs to do one of them—preferably getting to the deep structure of the information literacy concept your lesson is getting at—well.

QUESTION 3. IS THIS TECHNOLOGY ACCESSIBLE?

As we discussed in chapter four, inclusiveness is a critical component of learner-centered pedagogy. In terms of technology, inclusiveness can take various forms, which we broadly call accessibility. Typically, in the digital realm, accessibility refers to whether people with disabilities can successfully use and engage with a technology. So, one key consideration for selecting learner-centered library technology is compliance with accessibility standards. While federal agencies are bound by law (Section 508) to make all their information technologies available to disabled users, only some states have similarly toothsome policies, and private entities are not required to comply at all.[3] All of which is to say that we can't take for granted that any technology will work for all our students, especially those who have learning differences.

The World Wide Web Consortium (W3C) provides a consistently updated set of guidelines for web accessibility—inspired by the UN Convention on the Rights of People with Disabilities, which states that access to information is a basic human right—that is fully in compliance with the Americans with Disabilities Act (ADA).[4] Requirements on these guidelines range from having all images include an alternative descriptive tag, so that visually impaired users can access information about images, to providing keyboard access for critical functions of a website or digital tool, allowing individuals who are challenged by fine motor control to use them. Accessibility guidelines generally address the physical barriers that might prevent individuals from using tools but typically do not take other factors into consideration.

To address this, the learner-centered librarian also needs to consider accessibility in another way, via the question of whether students across the socioeconomic spectrum can access these tools. Does the tool require the purchase of a piece of hardware for it to be used? Growing numbers of students on university campuses experience food insecurity, often having to make a choice between a day's worth (or more) of meals and a textbook. Asking learners to purchase another device for class may create undue financial hardship. Does the tool require a fast computer or recent technology to function? Many students have old computers or cheap models, like Chromebooks, that don't have extensive memory or even the ability to download software. If you do determine that it's completely necessary to incorporate this cutting-edge technology into your instruction, then it's important to make sure that any hardware is available to be circulated and any software has been installed on library machines for students who may not otherwise have access. Keeping these factors in mind ensures that all students can participate fully in the learning process without feeling prevented from being able to engage or being shamed or embarrassed by their personal circumstances.

Let's turn to our research-topic worksheet one final time. By printing the flowchart, you make it accessible to any student, regardless of their technological savvy or personal device. You can also make it available to students who are not physically present in the same place at the same time by uploading it as a PDF to a course guide, learning management system, or other web-based repository. One thing to keep in mind in terms of accessibility, though, is the students' background knowledge of other tools—the ones that will allow them access to the tool you want them to engage with. For example, if you upload the PDF worksheet to the learning management system (e.g., BlackBoard), but none of your students typically use it and know how to access it, then you have created a crisis, and they will be distracted from your core learning goal by this semi-extraneous step. So it's critical to consider what your students already know—and not just about the course content.

Finally, let's imagine you have found a technological tool that is learner-centered and helps you solve a pedagogical problem, but it's not accessible in some way. In that case, since not necessarily a huge number of technologies would meet these conditions, it may be worth your while to figure out if there is a way to overcome the accessibility barrier. Is there a work-around or simply extra work to be put in so that a tool has an accessible version (e.g., adding alternative text to slides)? Can you propose that the library or other campus partners invest in purchasing equipment that would make a tool available to all students? Can you reach out to the tool's creators and state your case to make the tool accessible? Tools that unreservedly meet the previous two conditions set out in this chapter are uncommon enough that it's worth trying to remedy the situation if this question is the only one to which the answer is no.

We've proposed these questions in the order that we feel models a learner-centered process, from defining the problem to implementing a solution. To be sure, a "no" at each step of the process can be a deal breaker, but the last question has more leeway because you might be able to make something accessible, given the right resources and motivation. To summarize this section, we've created a handy flowchart that can serve as a quick reference for technological decision making in the information literacy context.

But Is It Learner-Centered? Five Case Studies

Now that we've created a framework for decision making related to technology, we examine the use of several popular technologies employed in libraries as case studies.

Before we get started, a word of caution and encouragement: While we conclude that some of these technologies may not fit within a learner-centered approach to library instruction, this does not mean that if you've used these tools, you've done something deeply wrong or should feel badly about your teaching. Even those of us who consistently sally forth into the classroom with an explicitly learner-centered focus can make missteps, in the realm of technology and pretty much anywhere else. Dani will admit to having used all the technologies highlighted here, some more extensively than

FIGURE 6.1
TECHNOLOGY SELECTION FLOWCHART

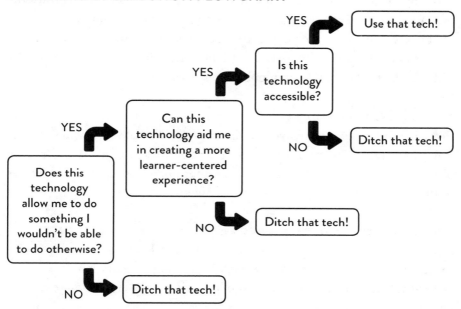

others, some in more learner-centered ways than others. Some of them she continues to incorporate into her practice, and some she has jettisoned. The most important thing is to constantly question and reflect on teaching methods. Sometimes you won't know if a tool works in the way you expect until you try it in the classroom. Trial and error is absolutely part of the process (and you know how much we love process!).

So, with that caveat in mind, let's get to examining five technological tools as case studies for transferring learner-centered principles to the use of new technologies in library instruction.

PREZI

What is it?

Several years ago, a new web-based presentation program called Prezi became all the rage. It was billed as a disruptor to the traditional presentation style—finally a way to eliminate the ubiquitous "death by PowerPoint." The program allows presenters to place their information on an infinite canvas, zooming in and out to display information. One of Dani's favorite professors in grad school referred to it as "the favored presentation tool of eight-year-old boys who like to make people nauseous" because of the program's capacity to spin, twist, and zoom between frames (i.e., what we typically consider slides in the traditional desktop publishing environment).

How is it used in libraries?

Prezi is used as an alternative presentation tool, usually replacing PowerPoint or Keynote. Some instruction librarians use Prezi in their in-person library sessions as part of their lecture. Other librarians use screen captures of Prezis to create asynchronous tutorial videos.

Does it pass the learner-centered test?

No. In fact, Prezi fails all three of our questions, making it a nonviable choice for learner-centered practitioners, regardless of implementation.

Firstly, Prezi does not pass the test of providing a novel solution to a problem. Many proponents of Prezi point to its perceived ability to present information in a nonlinear way as the key advantage over tools like PowerPoint or Keynote. However, while the program allows you to whiz and twirl between frames, it is still confined by the narrative constraints of presentation. It does not do anything fundamentally different from any other presentation tool but simply is wrapped in a new skin. The Prezi website proclaims increased audience engagement with the tool, but the evidence cited is about how people respond better to visuals than to text in general.[5] While the empirical evidence certainly supports that people process images faster than words, this isn't unique to Prezi. In fact, creating slide decks consisting primarily of images is a best practice for any presentation tool. The problem that this tool purports to solve—having people pay attention to a presentation—is one with many possible solutions, including no-tech ones (e.g., incorporating narrative), so there is no compelling reason to adopt something with more bells and whistles, like Prezi.

Even more importantly, Prezi does not help do anything more learner-centered in the classroom context. In a library session that includes lecture, using this tool over any other does not inherently create additional student engagement—it's up to the instructor to stop and ask questions, build a narrative, introduce a problem to solve, and apply other best practices that we've identified in this book. If anything, the movement and novelty of the Prezi may distract from the content that we want students to focus on learning.

Some practitioners may try to incorporate Prezi into an active-learning activity, asking students to create a presentation to demonstrate their understanding of a concept. In chapter three, we discussed how people remember what they pay attention to, and that is certainly a relevant consideration here. If Prezi is a new tool for your students, and they have to spend mental energy to learn how to use it, that's attention they're paying to the tool instead of to the information literacy ideas that you'd like for them to engage with.

Finally, Prezi is not accessible to learners with various types of disabilities. One major issue with Prezi is that screen readers are not able to interpret the content in a presentation, so individuals with visual challenges are unable to engage with Prezi presentations. While there are workarounds for this, such as exporting the frames to a PowerPoint presentation and adding alternative text in the notes section, Prezi has no native affordances for providing access to users with disabilities.

Prezi is a great example of a technology that on the surface looks like it could transform our practice but, upon closer examination, we find does not live up to expectations.

CLICKERS

What is it?

Though they've been around for well over a decade now, clickers (also known as classroom response systems) continue to be lauded as an emerging tool for active learning and classroom engagement. Students borrow or purchase individual electronic devices that allow them to respond to questions posed in class, either for practice or for a grade. These devices rely on radio or infrared signals to transmit responses to a central unit that collects the answers, using essentially the same technology as a television remote. Because of this technological limitation, most clickers are optimized for multiple-choice questions, with a few next-generation options (including smartphone apps) that allow for free-text answering of questions. Responses can be tied to student identity or made anonymous, and instructors can choose to display aggregate results to the class for further discussion.

How is it used in libraries?

Clickers are used in library instruction in much the same way that they are used in disciplinary lecture halls. Instructors tend to use clickers in two main ways: to check for understanding and to poll students.

Checking for understanding typically looks something like a quiz. The instructor poses a multiple-choice question that relates to content or concepts discussed in class or assigned in homework. The instructor receives the student responses in real time so the class can discuss the answers or even adjust the day's lesson based on demonstrated student need. Student answers may be simply informative or used for a grade (either participation or accuracy).

Instructors may also use clickers to poll students on topics without a specific correct or incorrect answer. Because polling-type questions require less creativity and strategy to create, they can be both created and implemented in class, allowing for on-the-fly opportunities to survey students.

Does it pass the learner-centered test?

Maybe, depending on the implementation. Clickers are often pointed to as a fantastic tool for encouraging active learning, and at least at the surface level, that's true: students must think about their answer choice and then (actively) press the appropriate button on their clickers. But what we really want students to do in active learning is practice the deep structure of concepts as we discussed in chapter three. So, the efficacy of the active-learning piece is highly dependent on the types of questions that are posed to the students via clickers and how those questions are addressed later.

Let's take the checking-for-understanding function here first. Just like any quizzing-type scenario, a huge variety of types of questions can be asked, ranging from regurgitating content to applying concepts in new ways. Asking students questions about whether they remember specific course content certainly gets at the retention half of the learning equation, but it does not incorporate transfer. Application questions, on the other hand, ask for students to both recall information and use it in a novel context. In this way, asking clicker questions can function as practice of deep structure. Critically, though, simply asking the understanding questions is not enough—the librarian also needs to give feedback to learners on why an answer was correct. There are multiple ways to do this: ask students to explain their answers to one another in small groups, demonstrate the thought process leading to a correct answer at the front of the room, or ask for volunteers who selected each answer to explain why they chose their answer. For a learner-centered instructor, it's not enough to simply state that a solution is incorrect; there must be an opportunity for students to receive real-time feedback and examine their process.

Next, let's examine the use of the polling function. This allows for library instructors to ask students to express their thoughts about content or organization of the class. This can be a powerful way to allow students to exercise some autonomy about class content and delivery, especially in a large class setting. There is some emerging evidence that, when students are presented with a choice of methods for learning, both conceptual learning and engagement tend to increase.[6] So, using clickers at the beginning of class to poll students on preferred methods of instruction could be a strategic way to increase both engagement and autonomy. Once again, questions need to be carefully framed so that the potential options for students still meet all our learner-centered criteria, but when done a thoughtful way, clicker polling can absolutely be learner-centered.

Now that we understand how clickers could be used, let's consider the problem context. In a large classroom setting, it may be challenging for a librarian to check in with individual students for understanding (if they can even squeeze through the rows in a lecture hall!) or get more than a handful of students to participate. An audience-response device can be a very useful tool for setting the expectation of 100 percent participation as well as for taking a pulse of the class on understanding course content. So, in a class of fifty or more students, clickers are one solution for solving issues with audience engagement and feedback. However, in a smaller session, using clickers may be more of a distraction than a helpful tool. Since we know that individual connection is so important for learning, we would want to take the route of relationship building with students whenever possible. Using this type of technology does put one more layer between the instructor and the student, so it would likely be counterproductive in a scenario where the librarian could personally engage with individual students. Clickers can solve the very particular problem of engaging with large classes, but they don't necessarily provide a solution for every type of engagement issue.

Cost, of course, is a major concern with clickers. A typical clicker usually costs around fifty dollars, which is typically paid by the students. If students are required to purchase clickers for other courses, then the librarian should employ the same tools already being used on campus and not burden students with additional costs. If clickers or audience-response devices are not required elsewhere on campus, then the question of access falls firmly with the library instructor. Possible options for providing access are purchasing an audience-response system specifically for library instruction (i.e., students borrow the clickers only while in the library, which precludes identity-tied quizzing without a large investment of time) and investigating free or "freemium" (with the subscription costs paid by the library) alternatives to clickers that work through the devices students already own. Current examples of these technologies include Kahoot! and PollEverywhere, but this is an emerging market.

Clickers, then, can serve a learner-centered function, but that doesn't necessarily mean that they always will. Whether this tool could be considered learner-centered depends heavily on how the library instructor implements it. It's also worth noting that clickers' learner-centered uses we've called out here do take just as much, if not more, work in terms of class preparation—for example, if you opt to give students a choice in the method of instruction, then you have to be prepared for each of those options. Similarly, writing a question that requires application of knowledge is much more challenging to write than a question that simply asks students to recall information. This is very much in line with our discussions throughout this book that being learner-centered is not the easiest path, but one that pays off with authentic learning for students.

RESEARCH/COURSE GUIDES

What is it?

Research and course guides are the digital children of the traditional paper-based bibliographies or pathfinders. Early in the 2000s, many libraries hard-coded guides onto their web pages in a variety of styles, but today there are multiple products on the market (most notably, SpringShare's LibGuides) that allow for the easy creation of online guides through a content management system–style interface.

How is it used in libraries?

Just like bibliographies and pathfinders, research and course guides are typically used as supplements to reference and instruction, although occasionally they are used as a replacement for these interactions. Librarians usually include resource recommendations tied to a specific course or discipline, and some include suggestions for research strategies or tools, such as citation management.

Does it pass the learner-centered test?

Maybe, depending on its implementation. There is a large subgenre out there of "bad LibGuides," which usually means that they include an overwhelming amount of information, are organized in a confusing way, or incorporate hard-to-read stylistic choices.

The path to bad LibGuides starts from the same place that a learner-centered implementation would: creating an online guide allows you to do something that you otherwise would not, namely, include a boatload of information that wouldn't fit into 50 (or 80 or 120 . . .) minutes. Research guides that are packed to the brim with resources technically pass our first question about allowing librarians to do something they would not be able to do without the technological tool, but the use of guides in this way falls apart when we start to consider their learner-centeredness.

Specifically, research and course guides that focus on resources without relating them to an acceptably narrow context, and that are not process oriented, violate almost all the principles that we've talked about in this book. A massive guide cognitively overwhelms the learner (as we discussed in chapter three), and without a specific context provided for why a student may be interested in exploring any of the resources listed in the guide, there's no perceived imperative to pay attention to it.

Perhaps counterintuitively, providing students with too many resources can limit the autonomy they're able to exercise. As we discussed in chapter one, one of the primary functions Rogers imagines for the learner-centered teacher is provision of resources. Especially for novice students, circumscribing the world of resources can actually help learners focus on the concepts, skills, and process that matter more than a complete understanding of all the resources out there that might apply to a given research topic.

However, we can certainly imagine and have seen, and created, course guides that are learner-centered. A research guide can act as a digital surrogate for an in-person interaction, by guiding students through the research process in an analogous way to what a librarian might do in an in-person setting. This might mean including questions for reflection that focus on significant learning, organizing the guide by waypoints in the research process, and including a subset of relevant resources for student needs.

Any accessibility concerns with online guides are relatively easily overcome by adding descriptive alternative text tags to any images in the guide, including multiple navigation options, and avoiding plug-ins that are not screen-reader friendly. Many proprietary software offerings, including LibGuides, will even prompt users to take these accessible actions throughout the creation process. And for students who might not have Internet access, there are usually ways for the librarian to print pages from the guide for at-home reference.

By following the same guidelines for creating a research guide that we've outlined for thinking about any instruction or reference interaction, it is absolutely possible to create and use research and course guides in a learner-centered way. Once again, the key is for the library practitioner to deliberately consider the needs of the learners and not default to creating an exhaustive bibliography. While there is certainly a place for those in academia, especially for very advanced researchers, these are typically not the people whom course guides are created for.

FLIPPED CLASSROOM TECHNOLOGY

What is it?

In the past five years, the "flipped classroom" has become one of the biggest trends in American education. The general idea behind the concept is that it flips the traditional in-class/homework dichotomy: instead of having students learn concepts in class via direct instruction (such as lecture) and practice those concepts themselves as homework, the flipped classroom model asks students to initially learn material on their own time, most commonly via videos, and then uses classroom time for students to practice the concept with the teacher providing expert, just-in-time feedback.

How is it used in libraries?

Academic librarians use the flipped classroom model, heavily relying on video capture technology, in much the same way that educators in any setting might—to free up time in the classroom to do something else. Whether that's to learn more content, demonstrate proficiency in the skills from the out-of-class video, or actually conduct research, it varies greatly depending on the librarian and the context.

Does it pass the learner-centered test?

Maybe, depending on its implementation.

At first glance, it seems like flipped classrooms would always be learner-centered; after all, isn't one of the critical aspects of learning (transfer) best learned in a setting where learners can immediately receive substantive feedback from an expert?

In its purest form, that's exactly what a flipped classroom does. However, the execution does not always lead to that. Let's consider our first metric: Does the flipped classroom allow you to do something that you might not otherwise be able to? In almost every case, the answer will be yes; if nothing else, the flipped classroom opens up time in the in-person session because students will ostensibly have already learned (or at least seen) certain skills and concepts via the video.

Issues can arise with both the video (or other alternative media for out-of-class learning, but we refer to it as video for ease of reference) and the in-class session itself. Basically, the video is a digital surrogate for whatever the instructor would have normally done in class. That might be a straight lecture, worked examples, or other semi-traditional methods of instruction. Because of the nature of video and asynchronous learning, it has to be a one-way interaction; there's no way for instructors to modify their approach based on learners' physical or verbal feedback. That makes the method of content delivery, as well as the content itself, more critical than ever. To be effective, the video should consider the same strategies that we've outlined in this book, from limiting learning outcomes to focusing on process. Likewise, the content of the video will also need to be learner-centered in nature for this method to be considered learner-centered as a whole. For example, a flipped classroom video about evaluating sources might say something like, "Good sources are scholarly in nature, published in peer-reviewed journals, and found in library databases," which is a pretty controlling and limited way of presenting the idea of "good" sources. Instead, a video that incorporates learner-centered approaches might include narration like,

> Determining whether a source is "good" for your project will depend on the nature of your research. In many cases, you will want to consult scholarly works, published by experts in repu-table sources, to support your argument and offer evidence. But in other cases, you may need to consult more nontraditional sources, such as blogs or websites, to present a full picture of the conversation about your topic. Thinking critically about the types of sources that will help you answer your research ques-tion is important for determining what might be "good" for you.

These two hypothetical videos will send learners in two very different directions, which illustrates that the content itself has to be learner-centered.

As for the in-class time, the temptation is always to use this new-found time to teach students more. But this is exactly where the implementation of flipped classroom technology tends to fall apart. It's only when classroom time is spent explicitly practicing the concepts presented in the out-of-class video in a new way, and when instructors can provide feedback to students on their utilization of these skills, that significant learning is achieved. In the language of this book, the in-class portion of the flipped classroom is a moment for students to demonstrate both retention and transfer, with the help of their instructors' feedback.

Accessibility is absolutely important to the whole flipped classroom idea, with the out-of-class portion almost always relying on computer technology. In the K–12 setting, more and more school districts are handing out Chromebooks or iPads and vouchers for free or discounted home Internet precisely so that students will have the tools they need to fully participate in a flipped classroom, regardless of their family's socioeconomic situation. So for librarians considering incorporating this method into their practice, it's important to consider whether all your students will have equal and consistent access to the tools they'll need as well as the background knowledge to use these tools effectively.

CHAT TOOLS

What is it?
Chat is a relatively simple web-based technology, leveraging instant messaging tools that have been around for almost two decades. Many e-commerce sites employ chat services to provide customers with support around the clock.

How is it used in libraries?
Chat tools are primarily used in libraries to provide reference services. Some libraries staff their own instances of chat, only available during their open hours, while other libraries band together to provide 24/7 consortial chat service to all their users. Implementation differs based on individual library websites, ranging from chat widgets that appear on various pages of the website to chat boxes that automatically pop up for users after 15 or 30 seconds on the library home page.

Does it pass the learner-centered test?
Yes!

Chat reference certainly provides a novel solution for a significant problem in contemporary librarianship: How do you reach patrons who need help outside of normal business hours, who are geographically remote, or who are just too shy to come up to the reference desk? Providing a web-mediated interface can help provide a solution for all these issues.

Just like any other reference interaction, the chat reference interview tends to be about a specific individual's specific information need. This heavily relies on the librarian immediately developing a relationship with the patron and getting to the heart of the research need, to find a solution or a path that meets that particular person's need. So, if we consider reference to be a learner-centered service (spoiler alert: we do!), then we would also consider chat reference to be learner-centered. Of course, it would be possible to approach chat reference in a non-learner-centered manner, just like it's possible to provide in-person reference in a non-learner-centered way. But we would consider the impulse to provide point-of-need reference via chat to come from a learner-centered place.

Finally, we must consider accessibility. Chat is a tool that requires a device and an Internet connection of some kind, but it does not require a fast connection or a high-powered computer. On the scale of technologies that libraries may consider employing in the public services arena, chat reference is a lightweight choice that actually extends the accessibility of library services: Patrons who may be housebound or otherwise unable to get to the physical library space are still able to avail themselves of librarian services via chat.

Application Is Everything

It's not a coincidence that over half of the examples in this chapter do not conclusively draw a yes or a no to the question, Does this technology pass the learner-centered test? With almost every technology, the implementation matters more than the technology itself in whether something might be considered learner-centered. But perhaps that's no surprise after reading this book. Each choice you make in designing your instruction or your approach to reference depends on how you choose to transfer your understanding of learner-centered pedagogy to your particular context. Technology is no exception.

NOTES

1. R. Volti, Society and Technological Change, 6th ed. (New York: Worth Publishers, 2010).

2. With thanks to C. T. Miller, "The Application of Carl Rogers' Person-Centered Learning Theory to Web-Based Instruction." Annual Proceedings of Selected Research and Development Practice Papers Presented at the National Convention of the Association for Educational Communications and Technology 24, no. 1–2 (2001): 278–83, for inspiration.

3. "GSA Government-wide Section 508 Accessibility Program," Section508.gov, accessed September 20, 2016, www.section508.gov.

4. "Accessibility," W3C, accessed September 20, 2016, www.w3.0rg/standards/webdesign/accessibility.

5. "The Science of Effective Presentations," Prezi, accessed September 23, 2016, https://prezi.com/the-science.

6. A. Assor, H. Kaplan, and G. Roth, "Choice Is Good, but Relevance Is Excellent: Autonomy—Enhancing and Suppressing Teacher Behaviours Predicting Students' Engagement in Schoolwork," *British Journal of Educational Psychology* 72, no. 2 (2002), 261–78.

CONCLUSION

The Timelessness of Learner-Centered Pedagogy

As we conclude this book, we hope that you now agree that learner-centered pedagogy is much more than the latest trend in librarian circles. In fact, we suggest to you that learner-centeredness is not a trend at all, but a way of approaching librarianship that can change over time, as our understanding of what it means to be a person learning something evolves. While the specific answers to the central question of this book may not always be the same, as long as librarians continue to monitor the current literature on motivation and the science of learning and follow where the evidence takes us, the basic framework that we present here will continue to apply.

And, indeed, we think that a learner-centered orientation can have implications for work across the library profession, not just in reference and instruction. Let's imagine what a learner-centered ethos of librarianship might look like across five major components of library work:

Instruction: The learner-centered instruction librarian facilitates significant learning about information through authentic engagement with learners. Throughout the course of the instruction interaction, the librarian assists students in the process of developing research questions that matter to them and then uses his informational skills to help students find information they care about. The learner-centered librarian does not engage in classical conceptions of bibliographic instruction, instead encouraging students to explore the world of information and bring their previous experiences in finding information to bear in the new research context.

Reference: The learner-centered librarian conceives of reference as one-on-one instruction, so many of the same underlying ideas from instruction apply. The learner-centered reference librarian helps the learner develop a research question that matters to her and then builds skills to help the learner find and identify quality information to answer that question. In a more personal setting than the traditional classroom, the librarian is able to conduct a reference interview that aims to connect authentically with the learner and to guide her to a question and resources that matter to her. This learner-centered reference interview connects explicitly with the tradition of the counselor librarian, which we discussed in-depth in chapter five.

Outreach: The learner-centered librarian who engages with outreach recognizes that authentic connection is central to both her work and learner-centered pedagogy. By getting out of the library and into spaces where people are engaged with their everyday activities, be it work, leisure, or education, the librarian can build a deeper understanding of how his work can align with the needs of the individual. By meeting with individuals in a setting outside the semi-artificial context of the library, librarians can encounter the learner at the point of need, which can then inform other work being done in the library. It is critical for a learner-centered librarian to get out of the library, whether by visiting student or community clubs, providing reference services in nontraditional settings, or engaging with classes in an embedded model.

Collection Development: The learner-centered information resources librarian follows in the tradition of Ranganathan by explicitly holding the interests of the users of the collection in mind while making selection decisions. This might mean working closely with public-facing librarians to determine current areas of research interest, keeping abreast of news and developments affecting the community served, and providing opportunities for library users to make recommendations for the collection. A learner-centered library collection would be unique from every other library collection, reflecting the interests and needs of that library's specific population. The work of instruction and reference librarians is, in many cases, directly affected by the resources available to them, so a learner-centered ethos in collecting is critical for the success of a learner-centered library. Thus, a "good" collection is not one that a librarian might believe contains the "right" resources, but one that contains resources that are useful and relevant to users' distinct needs.

Cataloging: The learner-centered cataloger would approach his work through the eyes of the library user, investigating how individuals in their community search for research materials and creating resource metadata that reflects those preferences, biases, and experiences. For example, outdated Library of Congress subject headings might lead to users never finding certain resources, so the learner-centered cataloger would attempt to discover what other terminology might be used within their community and then create local records that facilitate discovery of those materials.

In each of these examples, authentic connection is central: between the librarian and the learner, as well as between the learner and their research. To achieve this, the librarian must not only have knowledge of educational resources and the world of information, but also be a certain type of person, one who has a genuine desire to understand the inner world of others. Just like the person-centered therapist, the learner-centered librarian must practice empathy as a way of being, holding the individual learner at the heart of her work.

As we strive toward a fully learner-centered practice of librarianship, we would consider a practical success to be expressing these interests and views to others, both within and without the library. Building community around this approach is a powerful way to transform our work and to practice an existential form of librarianship: we are learner-centered educators because we decide that is what we are.

As you go forward and adapt these ideas for your own contexts, we hope that you will share your ideas and continue to enrich and expand the profession's understanding that *who we are as people matters* for how we teach, how we learn, and how we engage with information and each other.

DIRECTIONS FOR FURTHER READING

For those of you who would like to pursue the literature on learner-centered pedagogy more in-depth, we've compiled a list of further reading including many sources that shaped the ideas in this book and can help you deepen your understanding of learner-centered practices. We know that there are a lot of resources listed here. If you only can read a few, we've put an asterisk (*) next to a couple of sources for each chapter that we think are the most impactful and approachable.

INTRODUCTION

*Brecher, D., and K. M. Klipfel. "Education Training for Instruction Librarians: A Shared Perspective." *Communications in Information Literacy* 8, no. 1 (2014): 43–49.

Davies-Hoffman, K., B. Alvarez, M. Costello, and D. Emerson. "Keeping Pace with Information Literacy Instruction for the Real World." *Communications in Information Literacy* 7, no. 1 (2013): 9–23.

Fallis, D. "On Verifying the Accuracy of Information: Philosophical Perspectives." *Library Trends* 52, no. 3 (2004): 463–87.

*Head, A. J. *Learning Curve: How College Graduates Solve Information Problems Once They Join the Workplace*. Sonoma, CA: Project Information Literacy, 2012.

Walter, S. "Librarians as Teachers: A Qualitative Inquiry into Professional Identity." *College and Research Libraries* 69, no. 1 (2008): 51–71.

CHAPTER ONE

WHAT IS LEARNER-CENTERED PEDAGOGY?

Hidi, S. E., and J. A. McLaren. "Motivational Factors and Writing: The Role of Topic Interestingness." *European Journal of Psychology of Education* 6, no. 2 (1991): 187–97.

Hidi, S., and K. A. Renninger. "The Four-Phase Model of Interest Development." *Educational Psychologist* 41, no. 2 (2006): 111–27.

Hole, G. T. *Thinking Well about What Matters.* Minneapolis/St Paul, MN: West, 1993.

Kreber, C., and M. Klampfleitner. "Construing the Meaning of Authenticity in University Teaching: Comparing Explicit to Implicit Theories." *Journal of Constructivist Psychology* 25, no. 1 (2012): 34–69.

*Mayer, R. E., and M. C. Wittrock. "Problem Solving." In *Handbook of Educational Psychology*, edited by P. A. Alexander and P. H. Winne, 287–304. New York: Routledge, 2006.

Ranganathan, S. R. *The Five Laws of Library Science*, publication series 2. Madras, India: Madras Library Association, 1931.

Rogers, C. R. "Empathic: An Unappreciated Way of Being." *The Counseling Psychologist* 5, no. 2 (1975): 2–10.

*Rogers, C. R. "Questions I Would Ask Myself If I Were a Teacher." *Education* 95, no. 2 (1974): 134–39.

Rogers, C. R., H. C. Lyon, and R. Tausch. *On Becoming an Effective Teacher: Person-Centered Teaching, Psychology, Philosophy, and Dialogues with Carl R. Rogers and Harold Lyon.* London: Routledge, 2013.

Silvia, P. J. "Interest—The Curious Emotion." *Current Directions in Psychological Science* 17, no. 1 (2008): 57–60.

Patall, E. A. "Constructing Motivation through Choice, Interest, and Interestingness." *Journal of Educational Psychology* 105, no. 2 (2013): 522–34.

CHAPTER TWO

CURIOSITY AND LEARNING:
THE IMPORTANCE OF AUTHENTICITY AND AUTONOMY

Assor, A. "Allowing Choice and Nurturing an Inner Compass: Educational Practices Supporting Students' Need for Autonomy." In *Handbook of Research on Student Engagement*, edited by S. Christenson, A. L. Reschly, and C. Wylie, 421–39. New York: Springer US, 2012.

Assor, A., H. Kaplan, and G. Roth, "Choice Is Good, but Relevance Is Excellent: Autonomy-Enhancing and Suppressing Teacher Behaviours Predicting Students' Engagement in Schoolwork." *British Journal of Educational Psychology* 72, no. 2 (2002), 261–78.

Bonnett, M., and S. Cuypers. "Autonomy and Authenticity in Education." In *The Blackwell Guide to the Philosophy of Education*, edited by N. Blake, P. Smeyers, R. D. Smith, and P. Standish, 326–40. Malden, MA: Blackwell, 2003.

*Deci, E. L., and R. Flaste. *Why We Do What We Do: Understanding Self-Motivation*. New York: Penguin Books, 1996.

Deci, E. L., H. Jang, and J. Reeve. "Engaging Students in Learning Activities: It Is Not Autonomy Support or Structure but Autonomy Support and Structure." *Journal of Educational Psychology* 102, no. 3 (2010): 588–600.

Deci, E. L., R. Koestner, and R. M. Ryan. "Extrinsic Rewards and Intrinsic Motivation in Education: Reconsidered Once Again." *Review of Educational Research* 71, no. 1 (2001): 1–27.

Kernis, M. H., and B. M. Goldman. "A Multicomponent Conceptualization of Authenticity: Theory and Research." In *Advances in Experimental Social Psychology*, vol. 38, edited by Mark P. Zanna, 283–357. San Diego, CA: Academic Press, 2006.

Klipfel, K. M. "Authenticity and Learning: Implications for Reference Librarianship and Information Literacy Instruction." *College and Research Libraries* 76, no. 1 (2015): 19–30.

Medlock, G. "The Evolving Ethic of Authenticity: From Humanistic to Positive Psychology." *The Humanistic Psychologist* 40, no. 1 (2012): 38–57.

*Reeve, J. "Why Teachers Adopt a Controlling Motivating Style Toward Students and How They Can Become More Autonomy Supportive." *Educational Psychologist* 44, no. 3 (2009): 159–75.

*Rogers, C. R. "To Be That Self One Truly Is: A Therapist's View of Personal Goals." In *On Becoming a Person: A Therapist's View of Psychotherapy*, edited by C. R. Rogers, 163–82. New York: Houghton Mifflin, 1961.

Ryan, R. M., and E. L. Deci. "Autonomy Is No Illusion: Self-Determination Theory and the Empirical Study of Authenticity, Awareness, and Will." In *Handbook of Experimental Existential Psychology*, edited by J. Greenberg, S. L. Koole, and T. A. Pyszczynski, 449–79. New York: Guilford Press, 2004.

CHAPTER THREE

EMPATHY AND THE SCIENCE OF LEARNING: LESSONS FROM THE COGNITIVE LITERATURE

Boyd, B. *On the Origin of Stories: Evolution, Cognition, and Fiction*. Cambridge, MA: Harvard Belknap, 2010.

Brown, P. C., H. L. Reedier III, and M. A. McDaniel. *Make It Stick: The Science of Successful Learning*. Cambridge, MA: Harvard University Press, 2014.

Cowan, N. "The Magical Mystery Four: How Is Working Memory Capacity Limited, and Why?" *Current Directions in Psychological Science* 19, no. 1 (2010): 51–57.

Doyle, T., and T. Zakrajsek. *The New Science of Learning: How to Learn in Harmony with Your Brain*. Sterling, VA: Stylus, 2013.

Pashler, H., M. McDaniel, D. Rohrer, and R. Bjork. "Learning Styles Concepts and Evidence." *Psychological Science in the Public Interest* 9, no. 3 (2008): 105–19.

Roediger, H. L., and A. C. Butler. "The Critical Role of Retrieval Practice in Long-Term Retention." *Trends in Cognitive Sciences* 15, no. 1 (2011): 20–27.

Spaulding, A. E. *The Art of Storytelling: Telling Truths through Telling Stories*. Lanham, MD: Scarecrow Press, 2011.

*Willingham, D. T. *Why Don't Students Like School? A Cognitive Scientist Answers Questions about How the Mind Works and What It Means for the Classroom*. New York: John Wiley and Sons, 2009.

*Willingham, D., and D. Daniel. "Teaching to What Students Have in Common." *Educational Leadership* 69, no. 5 (2012): 16–21.

CHAPTER FOUR

RELATIONSHIPS: THE HEART OF LEARNER-CENTERED PEDAGOGY

Beutel, D. "Teachers' Understandings of Their Relationships with Students: Pedagogic Connectedness." *The International Journal of Learning* 16, no. 3 (2009): 507–18.

Cain, D. J. *Person-Centered Therapies.* Washington, DC: American Psychological Association, 2010.

Cornelius-White, J. "Learner-Centered Teacher-Student Relationships Are Effective: A Meta-analysis." *Review of Educational Research* 77, no. 1 (2007): 113–43.

*Duncan, S. "Carl Rogers and Gloria—Counselling (1965) Full Session." YouTube video, 45:40. Posted May 14, 2003. www.youtube.com/watch?v=24d-FEptYj8.

*Fine, S. "Librarians and the Art of Helping." *The Reference Librarian* 28, no. 59 (1997): 77–91.

Frisby, B. N., and M. M. Martin. "Instructor-Student and Student-Student Rapport in the Classroom." *Communication Education* 59, no. 2 (2010): 146–64.

Gehlbach, H., M. E. Brinkworth, A. M. King, L. M. Hsu, J. McIntyre, and T. Rogers. "Creating Birds of Similar Feathers: Leveraging Similarity to Improve Teacher-Student Relationships and Academic Achievement." *Journal of Educational Psychology* 108, no. 3 (2016): 342–52.

Heim, C. "Tutorial Facilitation in the Humanities Based on the Tenets of Carl Rogers." *Higher Education* 63, no. 3 (2012): 289–98.

Horvath, A. O., and L. Luborsky. "The Role of the Therapeutic Alliance in Psychotherapy." *Journal of Consulting and Clinical Psychology* 61, no. 4 (1993): 561–73.

Maxfield, D. K. "Counselor Librarianship at UIC." *College and Research Libraries* 15, no. 2 (1954): 161–79.

*Rogers, C. R. "The Characteristics of a Helping Relationship." In *On Becoming a Person: A Therapist's View of Psychotherapy*, edited by C. R. Rogers, 39–58. New York: Houghton Mifflin, 1961.

*Ross, C. S. "The Reference Interview: Why It Needs to Be Used in Every (Well, Almost Every) Reference Transaction." *Reference and User Services Quarterly* 43, no. 1 (2003): 38–43.

CHAPTER FIVE
TRUSTING THE PROCESS: CULTIVATING A GROWTH MINDSET

Duckworth, A. L., C. Peterson, M. D. Matthews, and D. R. Kelly. "Grit: Perseverance and Passion for Long-Term Goals." *Journal of Personality and Social Psychology* 92, no. 6 (2007): 1087–101.

Duckworth, A. L., T. A. Kirby, E. Tsukayama, H. Berstein, and K. A. Ericsson. "Deliberate Practice Spells Success: Why Grittier Competitors Triumph at the National Spelling Bee." *Social Psychological and Personality Science* 2, no. 2 (2011): 174–81.

*Dweck, C. *Mindset: The New Psychology of Success*. New York: Random House, 2006.

Ericsson, K. A., R. T. Krampe, and C. Tesch-Römer. "The Role of Deliberate Practice in the Acquisition of Expert Performance." *Psychological Review* 100, no. 3 (1993): 363.

Gross, M., and D. Latham. "What's Skill Got to Do with It? Information Literacy Skills and Self-Views of Ability Among First-Year College Students." *Journal of the American Society for Information Science and Technology* 63, no. 3 (2012): 574–83.

Lin-Siegler, X., C. S. Dweck, and G. L. Cohen. "Instructional Interventions That Motivate Classroom Learning." *Journal of Educational Psychology* 108, no. 3 (2016): 295–99.

Lin-Siegler, X., J. N. Ahn, J. Chen, F. F. A. Fang, and M. Luna-Lucero. "Even Einstein Struggled: Effects of Learning about Great Scientists' Struggles on High School Students' Motivation to Learn Science." *Journal of Educational Psychology* 108, no. 3 (2016): 314–28.

Schraw, G. "Knowledge: Structures and Processes." In *Handbook of Educational Psychology*, edited by P. A. Alexander and P. H. Winne, 245–63. New York: Routledge, 2006.

Siegle, D., L. D. Rubenstein, E. Pollard, and E. Romey. "Exploring the Relationship of College Freshmen Honors Students' Effort and Ability Attribution, Interest, and Implicit Theory of Intelligence with Perceived Ability." *Gifted Child Quarterly* 54, no. 2 (2010): 92–101.

*Willingham, D. T. "Ask the Cognitive Scientist: 'Grit' Is Trendy, but Can It Be Taught?" *American Educator* 6, no. 2 (2016), 28–44.

CHAPTER SIX

THE LEARNER-CENTERED TECHNOLOGIST

*Henry, D. J. "Person-Centered Online Education: What Carl Rogers Has to Say to Teachers." In *Encyclopedia of E-leadership, Counseling and Training*, edited by V. C. X. Wang, 23–34. Hershey, PA: Information Science Reference, 2012.

Knowlton, D. S. "A Theoretical Framework for the Online Classroom: A Defense and Delineation of a Student-Centered Pedagogy." *New Directions for Teaching and Learning* 84 (2000): 5–14.

Miller, C. T. "The Application of Carl Rogers' Person-Centered Learning Theory to Web-Based Instruction." In *Annual Proceedings of Selected Research and Development Practice Papers Presented at the National Convention of the Association for Educational Communications and Technology*, edited by M. Crawford and M. Simonson, 278–83. Bloomington, IN: Association for Educational Communications and Technology, 2001.

*Miller, C. T. "Enhancing Web-Based Instruction Using a Person-Centered Model of Instruction." *Quarterly Review of Distance Education: Research That Guides Practice* 8, no. 1 (2008): 25–34.

Motschnig-Pitrik, R. "Person-Centered E-learning in Action: Can Technology Help to Manifest Person-Centered Values in Academic Environments?" *Journal of Humanistic Psychology* 45, no. 4 (2005): 503–30.

Motschnig-Pitrik, R., and B. Standl. "Person-Centered Technology Enhanced Learning: Dimensions of Added Value." *Computers in Human Behavior* 29, no. 2 (2013): 401–9.

Reisetter, M., and G. Boris. "What Works: Student Perceptions of Effective Elements in Online Learning." *Quarterly Review of Distance Education* 5, no. 4 (2004): 277–91.

Swaggerty, E. A., and A. D. Broemmel. "Authenticity, Relevance, and Connectedness: Graduate Students' Learning Preferences and Experiences in an Online Reading Education Course." *The Internet and Higher Education* 32 (January 2017): 80–86.

Walkington, C. A. "Using Adaptive Learning Technologies to Personalize Instruction to Student Interests: The Impact of Relevant Contexts on Performance and Learning Outcomes." *Journal of Educational Psychology* 105, no. 4 (2013): 932.

Kevin Michael Klipfel received his master's degree in philosophy from Virginia Tech, where he was subsequently a lecturer in moral, political, and existential philosophy. He received his MSLS from the University of North Carolina at Chapel Hill, where his master's research on authenticity, motivation, and information literacy learning won the Dean's Achievement Award for the Best Master's Paper of 2013 in the School of Information in Library Science. He has presented nationally on student motivation and learning, both in and outside the library profession, and has published articles on the application of humanistic and existential psychology to learner-centered information literacy learning in journals such as *College and Research Libraries* and *Reference Services Review*. He lives and works in Los Angeles.

Dani Brecher Cook is director of teaching and learning at University of California, Riverside. She holds an MSLS from the University of North Carolina at Chapel Hill and an AB in English Literature from the University of Chicago. She has published on information literacy pedagogy and learning technologies in *College and Research Libraries News*, *Reference and User Services Quarterly*, and *Communications in Information Literacy*. Dani has presented on the intersection of these two topics nationally at conferences such as that of ACRL, LITA Forum, LOEX, and the Library Technology Conference. Along with Kevin Michael Klipfel, Dani is a cofounder of *Rule Number One: A Library Blog* (www.rulenumberoneblog.com). Prior to becoming a librarian, Dani worked in the publishing industry.

INDEX